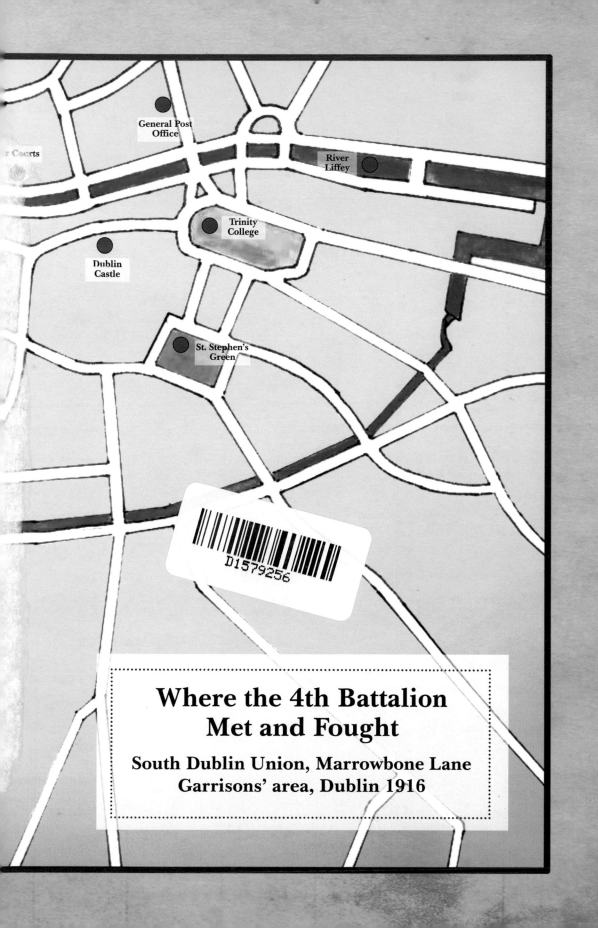

General Post
Office

River
Liffey

Trinity
College

Dublin
Castle

St. Stephen's
Green

r Courts

D1579256

Where the 4th Battalion
Met and Fought

South Dublin Union, Marrowbone Lane
Garrisons' area, Dublin 1916

Front Cover:

The Flag was hoisted over Marrowbone Lane Garrison by James Fitzpatrick.
Image reproduced courtesy of the National Museum of Ireland.

Sheila and Mollie O'Hanlon; photographs reproduced by kind permission of Ms. Kate Hayes and Ms. Rita Tapley.

William Dempsey release note from Knutsford Prison, May 1916.

Irish Volunteers, Members of the 4th Battalion, Dublin Brigade;
photograph reproduced by kind permission of the Pádraig Ó Broin Collection.

Back Cover:

The Nurses Building, South Dublin Union: image reproduced by kind permission of Prof. Davis Coakley, TCD Medical Centre, St James's Hospital and courtesy of the Brugha Collection.

Ireland First

Comóradh Ár Sinsir, 1916–2016
Relatives Remember

4th Battalion Dublin Brigade 1916

South Dublin Union – Marrowbone Lane Garrisons

Editors
Pádraigín Clancy and Clare Eager

Published 2016 by Cumann Gaolta – 4th Battalion Dublin Brigade 1916 Relatives Group,
South Dublin Union / Marrowbone Lane Garrisons.
© Copyright text: the Contributors except where indicated.
© Copyright image: the Contributors except where indicated.

The moral rights of the contributors have been asserted.
A catalogue record for this book is available from the British Library
ISBN: 978-1-78280-795-7

Map: With grateful appreciation to Niall Lowney.
Design by Siobhán O'Reilly, Great-Granddaughter of Peadar S. Doyle.
Printed and bound by Print Bureau, Inchicore, Dublin 8.

Contact the 4th Battalion Dublin Brigade Relatives: pclancy1916@gmail.com

Table of Contents

Dedication

"…none can deny the splendid courage of those who signed the proclamation of the Republic, of those who commanded the various positions which were occupied and finally of those who for a week stubbornly held the British Empire at bay…"[1]

Peadar S. Doyle
BMH Witness Statement 155
Member of "F" Company, 4th Battalion

Acknowledgements

The relatives and descendants of those who fought with the 4th Battalion at the South Dublin Union and Marrowbone Lane Garrisons (including Roe's Malting House and Watkins Brewery) wish to acknowledge the support of Dublin City Council, Diageo, Print Bureau, Inchicore, the Principal and Staff of Inchicore College of Further Education (for providing meeting room facilities for our group), St James's Hospital and TCD Medical Centre (especially Professor Davis Coakley), and the 1916 Relatives Association (especially John Stephenson and Ciarán O'Holohan).

As Co-Editors of *Ireland First: Comóradh Ár Sinsir 1916-2016*, we wish to acknowledge the assistance of the staff of the following institutions: Military Archives, Ireland, the National Library of Ireland, the National Museum of Ireland, the Irish Capuchin Provincial Archives, The Irish Folklore Collection and James Madigan, for his help in formulating our Questionnaire on 1916.

Thanks are due also to: Terry Moylan, Na Píobairí Uilleann; Niall Lowney for his artistic impression of the geographic layout of the South Dublin Union/Marrowbane Lane Garrisons' area. To Fr Paul Francis Spencer C.P., Mount Argus, for providing a photograph and information on the Passionist Fathers; Jessamine O'Connor, for allowing us to quote an extract from the poem *"Brothers – 7th May 1916"*; thanks also to Ray Bateson and Matt Doyle for their kind assistance; to Patrick Moloney, for proof-reading the entire document. Buíochas mór do Bhernardine Nic Giolla Phádraig, do Chaitríona Ní Bhuachalla agus do Éamonn Ó Riordáin scoláirí Gaeilge as ucht a gcuid cúnamh; agus don fhile Louis de Paor a thug caoincead dúinn a dhán 'An Glaoch' a fhoilsiú.

A special debt of gratitude is owed to members of our Group for their generous permission to reproduce individual histories, photographs and memorabilia and to Seán Tapley who took on the task of creating a pictorial archive.

~ ~ ~ ~

On a personal note I would like to thank my Co-Editor, Pádraigín Clancy, for her unwavering commitment throughout all stages of this project. A special note of thanks goes to my family and especially my sister, Evelyn Eager Quinn, for her proof reading skills.

On the occasion of the 100th anniversary of the Easter Rising we can, as descendants, be justifiably proud of all those who, in the words of their comrade Peadar S. Doyle, *'stubbornly held the British Empire at bay'*[2] in 1916.

Of such things is history made and here acknowledged.

Clare Eager
Co-Editor, April 2016

Leis seo thuas, mo bhuíochas óm chroí do chuile duine a ghlac páirt anseo, agus go háirid: do Clare Eager, mo Chomheagarthóir, gan a cuid oibre díograisí laethiúil, ní bheadh an tionscnamh seo déanta; do Chathal MacSwiney Brugha a thug misneach dom agus mé ag stracadh leis an saol; d'Oifig na nOibreacha Poiblí a thug sos dom chun na hoibre seo a thabhairt chun críche; do mo chairde dile in Éirinn agus in Árainn a sheasann liom i gcónaí, agus, faoi dheireadh do mo mháthair dhílis, Éibhlín, ós í atá fláithiúil agus foighdeach. Ar scáth a chéile a mhaireann muid!

Pádraigín Ní Sheachnasaigh Clancy
Comheagarthóir, Seachtain na Cásca 2016

Prologue

Maireann a gcuimhne fós in ár n-aigne[3]
Their memory lives on in our minds

There is a time for everything… and this is the time for remembering our ancestors and their heroic contribution to the birth of modern Ireland. The centenary year has been an extraordinary one marked by a strong camaraderie among us, probably stemming from a recognition that our ancestors fought together for Ireland's freedom in the 4th Battalion, Dublin Brigade, Irish Volunteers, under Commandant Éamonn Ceannt and Vice-Commandant Cathal Brugha. It is as if we know one another. Fate has woven us together.

Moments of serendipity have permeated throughout, such as: when, during our first visit to the Nurses building at St James's Hospital (formerly the South Dublin Union), three of the Brugha grandsons (Cathal, Fergus and Piaras) and David Ceannt (grandnephew of Éamonn) spontaneously sang *'God Save Ireland'*, just as Cathal Brugha had done as he lay severely wounded, in the same place, on Easter Thursday 1916; or, when Lorcan Dunne unexpectedly found a letter from his father Denis among the Pádraig Ó Broin family papers; or when my mother Eibhlín O'Shaughnessy Clancy met James Carberry, the grandnephew of her father's best friend Paddy O'Brien, killed in the Civil War, and showed him a memoriam card he had never seen but which she held in her late Father's prayer book; or when Clare Eager unearthed the flag which her grandfather James Fitzpatrick had raised in Marrowbone Lane; or when Con Colbert's nephew and grandnephew, Con and John, met the O'Hanlon cousins, Kate and Rita, whose aunts were in Marrowbone Lane with Colbert. Kate's mother had been named Connie after Con following a promise made by Kate's grandmother to Con Colbert that whether she had a boy or girl she would call the baby after him.[4] These are typical of the unforeseen moments which have been the hallmark of our coming together, proving the ancient Fianna adage that *'the music of what happens is the sweetest music of all'*.

The title *'Ireland First'* is the password given to my grandfather Theo O'Shaughnessy when reporting for duty to Marrowbone Lane on Easter Monday 1916. We chose it because it reflects the feeling which we know, as relatives, was in Volunteer hearts as they went 'out' in Easter Week. Unsurprisingly, it echoes, what was according to the 4th Battalion Volunteers, Éamonn Ceannt's song *'Ireland Over All'*.[5]

The publication begins with an introduction from local historian Cathy Scuffil, *Where the 4th Battalion Met and Fought*. Then, drawing the headings from our initial citation (already given) it continues with accounts of the leaders and of the rank and file Volunteer men and women – the latter in alphabetical order. All are written by a relative except in the case of WT Cosgrave, whose contribution has kindly been provided by Maurice Manning, a close friend of Liam Cosgrave, former Taoiseach, and son of WT.

Where we deemed it appropriate the editors have drawn from the Bureau of Military History witness accounts. Taken together, then, both family narrative and archival material provide a good insight into the activities of the 4th Battalion, Dublin Brigade, in Easter week 1916, and of the action at its garrison sites: South Dublin Union and Marrowbone Lane, including Roe's Malting House and Watkins Brewery.

The contributions also point to the formative influences of cultural nationalism (Conradh na Gaeilge) on the Volunteers. They also highlight the extraordinary level of mobilisation among the young (Na Fianna) and old at that time. Following the relatives' accounts there is a contribution on the Pipers Club, recollecting the musical legacy of Éamonn Ceannt and the 4th Battalion from Liberties musician Mick O'Connor.

The Epilogue *'It was hard to realise it was the last leave-taking'* includes extracts from Joseph Doolan, Annie Cooney, Lily O'Brennan and Fr Augustine Hayden OFM, Cap., on the last hours before the surrender at Marrowbone Lane and before the executions of 8th May 1916 in Kilmainham Gaol. This is followed by an extract from a poem *"Brothers – 7th May 1916"* – based on the words of Éamonn's brother, Richard – and composed by Jessamine O'Connor, great-grandniece of Éamonn Ceannt. Finally, recognising the fact that there is no definitive Roll of Honour of the men and women of the 4th Battalion we have included as complete a Centenary Roll of Honour as possible of all 4th Battalion members in 1916, which we have drawn from various sources. The publication also gives a pictorial record of the Volunteers submitted from our various family archives.

In conclusion, it must be said that the whole experience of coming together to commemorate our ancestors has been a unifying one in which those of us subsequently divided by Civil War have remembered and revisited the place where our ancestors stood together for Ireland during Easter week 1916. *Solas na bhFlaithis dóibh siúd atá imithe romhainn ar Shlí na Fírinne. I bparthas na nGrást go raibhimid…*

Pádraigín Ní Sheachnasaigh Clancy
Convenor – Relatives
4th Battalion Dublin Brigade 1916
Seachtain na Cásca 2016

*"The faculty of preserving
through centuries of misery,
the remembrance of lost liberty,
– this surely is the noblest cause ever man strove for,
ever lived for, ever died for."*

Roger Casement

Quoted by *Uachtarán na hÉireann* Michael D Higgins, Banna Strand,
1916 Centenary Commemoration, April 2016

CHAPTER 1

Before the Rising

Where the 4th Battalion Met and Fought

(See map on inside cover)

One hundred years ago, Dublin city's boundaries were marked by the Royal and Grand Canals and the areas beyond retained a rural character. Dolphin's Barn was a 'village in the city'. It had a long established history which was centered on the Old City Water Supply – a watercourse of the River Poddle. This passed through Larkfield Mills at Kimmage [now Ceannt Park] and on to Dolphin's Barn, then, under a long discreet laneway – known locally as the *'Back of the Pipes'* – which ended at Mountain View, Grand Canal Harbour, beside Guinness Brewey. The watercourse continued to the City Basin, near Pigtown at Basin Lane, which was close to the South Dublin Union [SDU]. The main gate to the SDU [now St James's Hospital] lay between McCaffrey's Orchard at Mount Brown and Pigtown.

The area around Dolphin's Barn was slowly developing into an urban landscape. Terraces of red-bricked houses such as at Dolphin Terrace along the desirable South Circular Road and squares, such as at Emerald Square were under construction. Yet, houses along Dolphin's Barn Street and Cork Street still retained yards to facilitate the keeping of horses and carts.

Beyond Emerald Square and Dolphin's Barn the land was given to market gardening at Fairbrothers, Sherrys and Flanagan's Fields, the latter named after Alderman Flanagan from Rialto. There were also larger farms such as at Portmahon House and Glenmalure House in Rialto and in parts of Kilmainham. Crossing the canal at Rialto Bridge brought one to Watery Lane, Brookfield Road. Here lay the Rialto gate to

the SDU with wards termed the Kilmainham Sheds directly inside the gate.

This, then, was the landscape where the men and women of the 4th Battalion met, trained and fought. They drilled at Larkfield Mills and Dolphin's Barn Brickworks. The iconic image of Pádraig Pearse, in full uniform, addressing the crowds of Conradh na Gacilge in 1915 took place at Towerfield House Ground, Dolphin's Barn, a site of assembly dating back to the Kings of Leinster.

The 4th Battalion was mobilised at Emerald Square Dolphin's Barn on Easter Monday, 24th April 1916 at 11.00 a.m. It was equipped with ammunition stored in Moggy Keogh's Yard opposite the Square. The women of Cumann na mBan had mobilised at 10.00 a.m. in nearby Weavers Hall and they then joined the men at Emerald Square.

Commandant Éamonn Ceannt with a dozen cyclists, followed by about thirty men on foot, proceeded by the *Back of the Pipes* to Mountain View and by the Grand Canal bank to Rialto Bridge, where they entered the SDU by a small door at the corner of Watery Lane. They took the keys and cut telephone wires, much to the astonishment of officials, who first thought they had embarked on parades and on drill practice. Once inside, most of the group was sent by Ceannt from the Kilmainham sheds at the Rialto gate towards the James's Street gate, half a mile away. Ceannt entrusted nine men under a Volunteer officer, [Captain George Irvine], with the defence of the Rialto gate. Fighting ensued during which Volunteer John Traynor and Nurse Margaret Keogh were killed by the British army. A second group, composed of about thirty men, under Cathal Brugha, proceeded along Grand Canal Harbour and entered the SDU by the James's Street entrance. The remaining parties proceeded respectively to Jameson's Distillery, Marrowbone Lane [under Captain Séamus Murphy]: to Watkins Brewery, Ardee Street [under Captain Con Colbert]; and to Roe's Malting House, Mount Brown [under Captain Thomas McCarthy]. Cumann na mBan [under Rose McNamara] were based at Marrowbone Lane only. Along with boys from Na Fianna, they carried messages about the various locations.

These sites were taken by the Volunteers with a view to preventing the British army entering into the city from Richmond Barracks in Inchicore, Islandbridge Barracks, Islandbridge and Wellington Barracks, South Circular Road, or from their Head Quarters at the Royal Hospital Kilmainham.

Cathy Scuffil
Local Historian

PH Pearse addresses crowd at Towerfield, Dolphin's Barn, 1915. Courtesy BMH.[6]

Letters to Mount Argus

Religious devotion is a hallmark of the participants of the 1916 Easter Rising, as the documents and personal memories reveal. The Passionist Fathers at Mount Argus were intimately bound up with the 4th Battalion. Many of the 4th Battalion Volunteers served mass there, some even on the morning of the Rising. Four priests stand out for their ministry to the Battalion; before, during and after the Rising. These were Fr Eugene

Standing at Mt Argus L-R : Fr. Joseph Smith, C.P., Mrs. Pearse, Margaret Pearse and Fr. Eugene Nevin, C.P.
Courtesy Passionist Archives.

Nevin, Fr Kieran Farrelly, Fr Joseph Smith and Fr Gerald O'Boyle. Fr Kieran heard the confessions of Pádraig and Willie Pearse, Éamonn Ceannt and Joseph Mary Plunkett on Good Friday night. He and Fr Eugene went to Marrowbone Lane to hear the confessions of the Volunteers. Fr Joseph promoted the Irish language with Mrs. Pearse and was the editor of "The Cross" which published Pádraig Pearse's poem *"A Mother Speaks"* in July 1916. Fr Gerald was Chaplain to the Men's Confraternity and the Pioneers at Mount Argus; this seems to be how he came into contact with the Volunteers.[7]

In his witness statement to the Bureau of Military History, Fr Eugene tells us that in the weeks prior to the Rising he had received a letter from Éamonn Ceannt thanking him for his words of encouragement to the Volunteers in a homily he had given.[8]

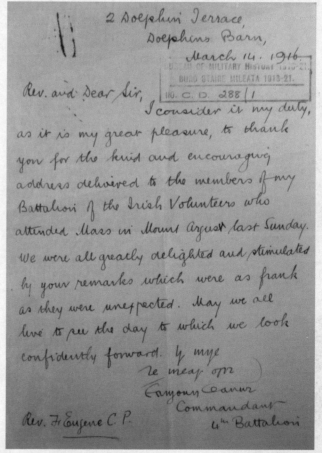

Letter from Éamonn Ceannt to Fr. Eugene Nevin, C.P., 14 March 1916.
BMH CD 288/1. Kind permission Military Archives.

Fr Eugene further relates that on Easter Sunday he received a letter by hand from Eoin MacNeill (via MacNeill's son) confirming the countermanding order. He then describes his reaction to the Rising on Easter Monday when he:

"was surprised and not a little shocked to hear and to see the Volunteers marching down the Kimmage and Harold's Cross Roads, on towards the city. I didn't know what to think, what to surmise, but all doubt was soon dispelled as news of the first clash of arms and sounds of rifle fire reached us. The Battle of Dublin, Easter Week, 1916, had begun…"[9]

Editors' Entry

POBLACHT NA H EIREANN.
THE PROVISIONAL GOVERNMENT
OF THE
IRISH REPUBLIC
TO THE PEOPLE OF IRELAND.

IRISHMEN AND IRISHWOMEN: In the name of God and of the dead generations from which she receives her old tradition of nationhood, Ireland, through us, summons her children to her flag and strikes for her freedom.

Having organised and trained her manhood through her secret revolutionary organisation, the Irish Republican Brotherhood, and through her open military organisations, the Irish Volunteers and the Irish Citizen Army, having patiently perfected her discipline, having resolutely waited for the right moment to reveal itself, she now seizes that moment, and, supported by her exiled children in America and by gallant allies in Europe, but relying in the first on her own strength, she strikes in full confidence of victory.

We declare the right of the people of Ireland to the ownership of Ireland, and to the unfettered control of Irish destinies, to be sovereign and indefeasible. The long usurpation of that right by a foreign people and government has not extinguished the right, nor can it ever be extinguished except by the destruction of the Irish people. In every generation the Irish people have asserted their right to national freedom and sovereignty; six times during the past three hundred years they have asserted it in arms. Standing on that fundamental right and again asserting it in arms in the face of the world, we hereby proclaim the Irish Republic as a Sovereign Independent State, and we pledge our lives and the lives of our comrades-in-arms to the cause of its freedom, of its welfare, and of its exaltation among the nations.

The Irish Republic is entitled to, and hereby claims, the allegiance of every Irishman and Irishwoman. The Republic guarantees religious and civil liberty, equal rights and equal opportunities to all its citizens, and declares its resolve to pursue the happiness and prosperity of the whole nation and of all its parts, cherishing all the children of the nation equally, and oblivious of the differences carefully fostered by an alien government, which have divided a minority from the majority in the past.

Until our arms have brought the opportune moment for the establishment of a permanent National Government, representative of the whole people of Ireland and elected by the suffrages of all her men and women, the Provisional Government, hereby constituted, will administer the civil and military affairs of the Republic in trust for the people.

We place the cause of the Irish Republic under the protection of the Most High God, Whose blessing we invoke upon our arms, and we pray that no one who serves that cause will dishonour it by cowardice, inhumanity, or rapine. In this supreme hour the Irish nation must, by its valour and discipline and by the readiness of its children to sacrifice themselves for the common good, prove itself worthy of the august destiny to which it is called.

Signed on Behalf of the Provisional Government,

THOMAS J. CLARKE.
SEAN Mac DIARMADA.   THOMAS MacDONAGH.
P. H. PEARSE.   EAMONN CEANNT.
JAMES CONNOLLY.   JOSEPH PLUNKETT.

CHAPTER 2

"The splendid courage of those who signed the Proclamation"

Éamonn Ceannt, Commandant, 4th Battalion

At Easter 1916, Éamonn Ceannt was living at Dolphin Terrace, Dolphin's Barn, with his wife Áine, and their son, Rónán. Born in Ballymoe, Co Galway on 21 September 1881, his father's promotion within the Royal Irish Constabulary brought the family initially to Co Louth, and later to Dublin. Éamonn, a bright scholarship boy, attended the Christian Brothers O'Connell School in Richmond Street. He worked in Dublin Corporation and remained a valued employee until Easter Week 1916. A member of the Dublin Metropolitan Officers' Association he was deeply committed to the right of workers to organise. Passionate about resurrecting the language and music of Ireland he joined the Gaelic League and learned the Uilleann pipes. In 1908, he famously played the pipes for the Pope in Rome.

Éamonn Ceannt

Ceannt became interested in finding a political solution to the question of Irish independence and initially joined Arthur Griffith's Sinn Féin. By 1911, however, Seán MacDiarmada had recruited him to the more radical, oathbound, Irish Republican Brotherhood (IRB). He was an enthusiastic founder of the Irish Volunteers on their establishment in 1913. At the head of the 4th Battalion, Ceannt was present when the Asgard entered Howth Harbour in April 1914. A week later he took part in a second armaments landing at Kilcoole, Co. Wicklow.

Following the outbreak of World War 1 in August 1914, Ceannt and certain members of the IRB decided to stage an insurrection to win independence for Ireland. He was appointed to the secret IRB Military Council with Joseph Plunkett, Patrick Pearse, and subsequently, Tom Clarke, Seán MacDiarmada and James Connolly. By early 1916 their plans were in place and the date of Easter 1916 had been secretly agreed. During Holy Week, Eoin MacNeill, Chief of Staff of the Irish Volunteers, belatedly discovered what the IRB Military Council was planning and issued a countermanding order late on Holy Saturday cancelling the scheduled mobilisation on Easter Sunday. The Military Council decided to defer the

Rising to Easter Monday with disastrous consequences for the Rising's chances of military success.

When the 4th Battalion met at Emerald Square on Easter Monday morning, the confusion meant that only c.120 Volunteers out of the Battalion's full strength of c.700 was available. En route to the South Dublin Union (now the site of St James's Hospital), the Battalion Companies took up positions at Marrowbone Lane Garrison, at Watkins Brewery and Roe's Malting House. During the week that followed the South Dublin Union became the site of fierce fighting. At all times it was under sniper fire from British troops. Ceannt and his men were entrenched in their headquarters in the Nurses' Home of the Union, but they had little news of what was happening elsewhere in the city or at the three other locations. On the Thursday, Cathal Brugha, Ceannt's second in command, was critically injured. At the end of the week, Éamonn Ceannt, under direct orders from the Provisional Government, reluctantly surrendered.

Following a series of secret military field courts martial, the fifteen rebel leaders were executed. Éamonn Ceannt, together with Con Colbert, Seán Heuston and Michael Mallin, was executed at daybreak on Monday, 8th May 1916. In a letter that he addressed to the people of Ireland, Éamonn Ceannt, uniquely among the leaders of the Rising, expressed his deep regret at being ordered to surrender. He advised future generations, *'never to treat with the enemy, never to surrender to his mercy'*. While acknowledging the kindness of individual British soldiers, he wrote:

"The enemy has not cherished one generous thought for those who, with little hope, with poor equipment, and weak in numbers, withstood his forces for one glorious week. Ireland has shown she is a Nation. This generation can claim to have raised sons as brave as any that went before. And in the years to come, Ireland will honour those who risked all for her honour at Easter in 1916."

Mary Gallagher
Grandniece

Postcard from Rome 1908: Signed by Éamonn Ceannt to his Mother in Law Mrs Brennan (Ceannt writes 'Played before his Holiness'). Courtesy National Library of Ireland.

Ceannt played the War Pipes before Pope Pius X on 24 September, 1908. The tunes he played included: O'Donnell Abú, The Wearing of the Green, I won't be a Nun (Information courtesy of Terry Moylan, Na Píobairí Uilleann)

CHAPTER 3

"Of those who commanded the various positions which were occupied"

Henry S. Murray

Writing some thirty years after the Rising, Henry S. Murray, (a Lieutenant in "A" Company, 4th Battalion) recalled the *distribution of the officer personnel and members of the various Companies of the Fourth Battalion (with the exception of "E" company)…during the 1916 Rising.*[10]

With regard to the South Dublin Union and Marrowbone Lane Garrisons, including Roe's Malting House and Watkins Brewery, Murray recorded that the complement of Leaders and Volunteers was as follows:

South Dublin Union
In addition to the officer command structure, of which there were 10, Murray stated that a further 65 Volunteers served in the South Dublin Union. They were led by:
- Commandant Éamonn Ceannt (Battalion Commandant)
- Vice-Commandant C. Brugha (Battalion Vice-Commandant)
- Lieutenant Seán McGlynn (Staff)
- Lieutenant G.F. Murray (Staff)
- Lieutenant W. Byrne (Staff)
- Lieutenant George Irvine (Captain "B" Company)
- Captain D. ffrench-Mullan (Captain "D" Company)
- 1st Lieutenant W.T. Cosgrave ("B" Company)
- 2nd Lieutenant W. Corrigan ("B" Company)
- 2nd Lieutenant L. O'Brien ("D" Company)

Marrowbone Lane Distillery
In addition to the officer command structure, of which there were 8, there were a further 105 Volunteers arranged in company formation, from "A" to "F". They were led by:
- Captain Séamus Murphy (Battalion Adjutant and Captain "A" Company)
- Captain Con Colbert (Captain "F" Company)
- Captain J. Kenny (Battalion Quartermaster)
- Lieutenant P. Cosgrave (Assistant Battalion Quartermaster)
- 1st Lieutenant H.S. Murray ("A" Company)
- 2nd Lieutenant S. O'Byrne ("A" Company)
- 1st Lieutenant J. McGrath ("D" Company)
- 1st Lieutenant C. O'Byrne ("F" Company)

Murray also recalled that Volunteers from Na Fianna Éireann, from "C" Company, 3rd Battalion, Irish Citizen Army and Cumann na mBan members led by Rose McNamara, all accounted for the remaining 32 who fought at this location.

Prior to evacuating **Roe's Malting House** and **Watkins Brewery**, a total of 18 Volunteers served at the former, under the command of 1st Lieutenant P. Egan, and 2nd Lieutenant C. O'Grady. It appears that Watkins Brewery was manned by 8 Volunteers only. Indeed, Murray wrote that,

"Early in Easter Week, 1916 the adjacent posts at Roe's Distillery and Watkins Brewery were evacuated by the units of the Fourth Battalion detailed to occupy these positions. The unit holding Watkins Brewery under Con Colbert reported in a body to Séamus

Murphy at Marrowbone Lane Distillery and many members of the garrison at Roe's Distillery reported individually. The garrison at Marrowbone Lane Distillery was further augmented by the arrival of many individuals from different units who had failed to report on Easter Monday morning for various valid reasons…"[11]

More recent studies suggest that, at best, the overall numerical strength of the 4th Battalion during Easter Week was in the region of 280, composed of 251 men and 29 women.[12]

Editors' entry

Cathal Brugha, Vice-Commandant, 4th Battalion

Rugadh Cathal Brugha ar an 18ú Iúil 1874. Ar scoil i gColáiste Belvedere dó bhí an-dúil aige sa snámh, sa dornálaíocht agus i roinnt spóirt eile. Chuaigh sé isteach i gConradh na Gaeilge i 1899. Is ansan a d'athraigh sé a ainm ó Charles St. John Burgess go dtí Cathal Brugha. Níos déanaí bhí sé ina Uachtarán ar Chraobh an Cheitinne.

In Easter 1916 Cathal Brugha was Vice-Commandant of the 4th Battalion, Dublin Brigade that held the South Dublin Union (now St. James's Hospital). In a British attack on the Nurses' Home he was hit by an exploding grenade and automatic pistol fire. Falling back seriously wounded, with 25 injuries from shrapnel and bullets, Brugha single-handedly held his position, even though his comrades had retreated, presuming the position was lost. Late that night, when the British soldiers had withdrawn, his comrades heard his voice ringing out the song 'God Save Ireland' and went to his rescue. They were able to staunch the loss of blood. It was believed that he would die as a result of his wounds. Vol. John Joyce later stated,

'Only for the extraordinary heroism of our Vice-Commandant, Cathal Brugha when seriously wounded, all would be lost. It was his almost single handed resistance and his inspired singing of 'God Save Ireland' at a critical moment that raised our little garrison to its greatest effort which finally repulsed this final British assault.'

Brugha recovered, but was left with a limp. On release from hospital he re-organised the leadership of the Irish

Cathal Brugha

Volunteers and the Citizen Army into a single force. At a Sinn Féin Convention in 1917 he proposed a Republican Constitution, which was unanimously accepted. He was also elected Chief of Staff of the Volunteers. In 1918 he was elected as a Sinn Féin TD and in de Valera's absence in 1919, Brugha presided over the first meeting of Dáil Éireann as its acting President. He was elected as Minister for Defence. He proposed an Oath of Allegiance to the Irish Republic for the Deputies, the Irish Volunteers and any others who, in the opinion of An Dáil, should take the same oath.

Bhí sé i gcoinne an Chonartha, ag rá le linn na ndíospóireachtaí: *'Nach dtuigeann sibh, má shíníonn sibh é, go mbeidh sibh ag scoilt Éire ó bhun go barr?'* Chaith Brugha an dá mhí deiridh dá shaol ag iarraidh an deighilt a leigheas, agus an arm a choinneáil faoi údarás na Dála.

Cathal Brugha was survived by his wife, Caitlín Kingston, their five daughters: Nollaig, Nóinín, Brenda, Fidelma, Nessa; and one son, Ruairí.

Cathal MacSwiney Brugha
A Gharmhac

Con (Cornelius) Colbert, Captain, 4th Battalion

Con Colbert was born on 19th October 1888 in Moanleana, Castlemahon, Co. Limerick. The fourth youngest of thirteen children, the family moved to Galeview, Templeathea and he went to National School in Athea. His mother, Nora, died in 1892. At 15 he went to live with his sister, Catherine, in Ranelagh, Dublin, obtaining a job at Kennedy's bakery and working there until 1916.

Con came from a strongly Nationalist family. His father, Michael, had taken part in the Fenian rising of 1867. Con had a keen interest in Irish history and culture and became a member of the Gaelic League. He struggled learning Irish but persevered with help from Pádraig Pearse. He became a voluntary drill teacher at St Enda's school. He wrote poetry under the pen-name An Claidheamh – The Sword. He became a Captain in Fianna Éireann, training boys in physical fitness, military drill, rifle exercises, signaling, camping and first-aid. Self-discipline was encouraged and he himself never smoked, drank or swore. The uniform of his Fianna group was an Aran jersey and kilt. They earned a name for engaging with and stealing Union Jacks from the Baden-Powell scouts.

In 1913 he joined the Irish Volunteers and became a Captain in the 4th Battalion of the Dublin Brigade under Éamonn Ceannt. On Easter Monday, he cycled about, issuing orders for the men to assemble at 11am at Dolphin's Barn. Initially based at Watkins Brewery he and his men later moved to Jameson Distillery in Marrowbone Lane, which was under the command of Séamus Murphy. The Volunteers were

Con Colbert

deeply disappointed when the surrender order filtered through to them. They were marched to Richmond Barracks. Con was identified by his kilt uniform and singled out by the Dublin Metropolitan Police as being a strong activist. At his court martial, on 4th May 1916, he refused to answer any of the charges against him. Sentenced to death, he was moved to Kilmainham Gaol where he declined to see visitors but wrote letters to his family and friends. On the eve of his execution he sent for Mrs. Ó Murchadha, who was also a prisoner. According to her witness account he said he was *'proud to die for such a cause'*. Holding his Bible, he told her he was leaving it to his sister. He also handed her three buttons from his Volunteer uniform saying *'they have left me nothing else'*. He asked Mrs. Ó'Murchadha to pray for him and for the others who would be executed. The soldier who was guarding Colbert reputedly cried saying *'if only we could die such a death.'*

Con Colbert was shot at dawn on Monday, 8th May 1916, along with his fellow patriots Éamonn Ceannt, Michael Mallin and Seán Heuston. They were not afforded the dignity of a proper burial but, instead, were buried in a mass grave in Arbour Hill Prison. His death had a huge impact, especially in Limerick, where hundreds joined the Volunteers. His brother Jim, a farmer, having already followed Con's example in joining the Volunteers, became fully active in the War of Independence and Civil War. He was elected Sinn Féin TD for Limerick and later helped form Fianna Fáil.

**Con Colbert (Nephew),
John Colbert (Grandnephew)
Gerard Buckley, Agatha Barrett,
Athea, Co. Limerick**

In 1909 Countess Constance Markievicz took the first steps towards establishing **Na Fianna** with the help of Con Colbert and others. She recruited boys willing to work for the independence of Ireland. With the founding of the Volunteers in November 1913, the value of the work of the Fianna was immediately realised. Fianna drill halls throughout the country were utilised. Fianna Officers became Volunteer Officers (in many cases having higher rank in the Volunteers than in the Fianna).

During the Rising, Officers of Na Fianna commanded many positions: Na Fianna Chief, Countess Markievicz, was at the College of Surgeons; Con Colbert at Watkins Brewery and Marrowbone Lane Distillery; Seán

Members of Na Fianna drilling at St Énda's Fianna Hall, Rathfarnham, Dublin, before 1916. Con Colbert may be in picture. Courtesy John Colbert.

Heuston at the Mendicity Institution Usher's Island. Liam Staines, also at the Mendicity Institution, was badly injured there, while a party commanded by a Fianna Officer rushed the Magazine Fort in the Phoenix Park and made an almost successful attempt to detonate the explosives inside. This was to signal the start of the Rising. From here they withdrew to the Four Courts Garrison and endured some of the heaviest fighting.

We believe that Na Fianna Éireann have kept the military Spirit alive in Ireland during the past four years, and if the Fianna had not been founded in 1909, the Volunteers of 1913 would never have arisen.

P.H Pearse, February 1914

Editors' Entry

Fianna Camp Outside Dublin, (Con Colbert behind man on right in front row). Courtesy Fitzgerald collection, Military Archives.

William T Cosgrave and 1916 – 1st Lieutenant, 4th Battalion

William T Cosgrave was described by his son Liam as 'an extraordinary ordinary man' and by the English writer V.S. Pritchett as *'a perfect exemplar of the ordinary man suddenly elevated to high office who had the inborn moral character that is required for rule'*. And yet this ordinary man, who was always proud of his Dublin roots, was to become a major figure in Irish politics, the first head of an independent Irish government and more than any other figure helped establish, stabilise and develop the new State.

WT Cosgrave was born at 174 James's Street on 6 June 1880 where his father Thomas had a bar and grocery. He was educated by the Christian Brothers at James's St and later at the O'Brien Institute in Marino. After leaving school he ran the family business. His father Thomas had been involved in local politics before his early death and William followed his example. He was profoundly influenced by Arthur Griffith and attended the first national conference of Sinn Féin in 1905 and was elected to Dublin Corporation in 1909. He was an effective member with a particular interest in housing and in the scandal of the slums and was a strong advocate of the Irish language. He attended the inaugural meeting of the Irish Volunteers which he joined and became a lieutenant in "B" Company of the 4th Battalion under the command of Éamonn Ceannt. He was involved in the Howth gun running and helped store some guns for later use. When he heard of the mobilisation on Easter Monday he cycled to his battalion headquarters in Kimmage and found it was empty. He then joined the Battalion at Dolphin's Barn. A group of 120 men tried to occupy the vast sprawling South Dublin Union (now St James's Hospital). Cosgrave found himself working closely with Ceannt and Cathal Brugha. The strategic location of the Union enabled the rebels threaten but not disrupt British movements from Kingsbridge. It was at Cosgrave's suggestion that they used

William T Cosgrave

the night nurses home as their main defensive position. In the heavy fighting which followed Cosgrave's brother Gobban was shot dead by a sniper. By late Monday night the British had occupied all the buildings at the back of the institution while the Volunteers held those at the front, overlooking James's Street. This stalemate lasted for another six days.

After the surrender the prisoners were moved to Richmond Barracks and on 4th May Cosgrave was court martialled, accused of taking part in an armed rebellion. His trial lasted less than fifteen minutes. The verdict and sentence were 'Guilty. Death by being shot'. His brother Philip received the same sentence but both sentences were later commuted to life imprisonment. The rebels were released in June 1917 and shortly afterwards he was elected MP for Kilkenny. This was the beginning of over thirty years of parliamentary service during which time he served in various ministries alongside the man he admired most, Michael Collins. On Collins' death he became head of government until 1932 winning three general elections in the process.

Space does not permit discussion on his later distinguished career. When he died in November 1965 his great political rival Seán Lemass praised,

'the privations and the sacrifices which he endured so that national freedom might be ours, the capacity he displayed in presiding over the administration when responsibility was his, the grace with which he handed over responsibility when the people so willed, the dignity with which he carried out his duties as Leader of the Opposition and later, as a private member of this House, the generosity of spirit with which he lent his hand to the defence of the State in time of national danger.'

WT Cosgrave is buried in Goldenbridge Cemetery.

Maurice Manning
Biographer WT Cosgrave
and family friend

Séamus Murphy[15] Captain, 4th Battalion

In his Witness Statement to the Bureau of Military History Séamus Murphy recalled a few occasions when Éamonn Ceannt hinted to him of things to come. Murphy wrote:

"Some time at the beginning of 1916, or perhaps at the end of 1915, Commandant Ceannt hinted to me, as we walked home from a parade meeting, of the necessity to be prepared for serious work. Later on, coming towards St. Patrick's Day, I was speaking to him one evening and he was greatly perturbed. He told me definitely that Connolly wanted an immediate Rising. I think it would be about St. Patrick's Day 1916, and that they were having considerable trouble over the matter. Just about this time Ceannt had indicated a sort of general plan. He referred, as well as I remember, to the occupation of the South Dublin Union, and in particular to Marrowbone Lane, as our defensive posts. He was beginning to confide in me, without being too detailed, as to the serious work ahead.

I remember Éamonn Ceannt describing with enthusiasm how from the South Dublin Union we could control or stop the troops entering the city from Richmond Barracks. I am not prepared to state that he did not convey this information in a way which indicated that it would not apply at a particular time, but when the opportunity arose. He gave me the information but at the same time he did not indicate that it

Séamus Murphy

would come at a certain time, it was more a hypothetical situation. With regard to Marrowbone Lane his idea, as well as I remember, was that its occupation would control the situation if the troops attempted to use any by-road, such as Cork Street, they could be seen from the end of Marrowbone Lane. Also it overlooked the back of the South Dublin Union."[16]

Editors' Entry

Secrecy – At Muldoon's Tea Room

The secrecy surrounding the organisation of the Easter Rising was alluded to by my grandfather, **Patrick Egan**, in his statement to the Bureau of Military History. He related:

"About a fortnight or three weeks before Easter 1916 a gathering of all the officers of the 4th Battalion was held in Muldoon's (?) Tea room at Old Bawn on a Sunday evening. Captain McCarthy told me to meet him at Terenure which I did. After waiting a short while, we were joined by Willie Pearse. All three of us cycled to Old Bawn. In Muldoon's house there was a large room where we all gathered and had tea. At both ends of this room were two other smaller rooms. Tea over, we sat about, chatting and smoking. Not to my recollection was there any reference to the Rising, or a hint of it. Commandant Kent and Vice Commandant C. Brugha, with Willie Pearse, adjourned into one of the smaller rooms. They were in there practically all the evening after the tea was over. Kent would come out occasionally and hold a short conversation with one of the officers and then return. On one of these occasions he spoke to Captain McCarthy. I was called aside, and taken into the third (unoccupied) room. Kent said he heard from Tom that my brother (Joseph) had a powerful motorcycle (7/9 H.P. Harley-Davidson) and that they were looking for a man who wasn't known and who would be willing to carry out an important job. I said that I was sure he would be only too willing, but I was afraid he had little petrol (A British Military Order had placed restrictions on the sale and possession). To this, Kent smilingly replied, "Don't let him worry about that we have plenty of German Gold" and told me to get him to report to him at his home. I, at the time, was told nothing of his mission. We then went back to the big room, and the evening went on. What went on in the other room with Pearse, Kent and Brugha, one can only guess. The evening ended and, on approaching my brother, I found him, as I said, only too willing to take on any job."[17]

Patrick Egan, Grandson

Rose McNamara[18] Officer-in-Charge, Cumann na mBan

In her Witness Statement to the Bureau of Military History, Rose McNamara, the Officer-in-Charge of the Cumann na mBan members at Marrowbone Lane, wrote of the mobilisation as follows:

"On Easter Monday, April 24th, I was mobilised for Weaver's Hall, Cork Street, full uniform and equipment, for 10 o'clock a.m. We formed up outside the hall, 25 in number, where we marched to Emerald Square for orders from Commandant E. Ceannt; got order to follow Company of Volunteers just forming up. We marched behind until we reached the Distillery in Marrowbone Lane (used as forage stores for the British Government) at 12 o'clock. I next saw

Rose McNamara

Captain Murphy who was in charge of Volunteers, 4th Battalion, knock at small gate and demand same to be opened in the name of the Irish Republic. As soon as we got in prisoners were made of the Lodge-keepers, also a soldier in khaki. We remained in an old cellar all day, waiting for work to do. We heard heavy firing from both sides all the day. There were four workmen on the premises who were also made prisoners but were later blind-folded and were let out at dark. One slight casualty-P.McGrath-which we dressed with success. Firing continues till dark; reinforcements of 60 men arrive in the evening; towards evening two women bring us in some food, tea, etc., which we needed badly. We divided up into squads and posted ourselves in close touch with the different firing lines, and lay on sacks of oats or grains, which was very uncomfortable. M. Cosgrave, the Q.M., and myself were up very early to prepare some sort of breakfast for the men."[19]

Editors' entry

Letter written by Séamus Ó Murchadha on behalf of Rose McNamara, in connection with her application for a Military Pension. Extract from Military Service Pension Collection.

CHAPTER 4

"Of those who for a week stubbornly held the British Empire at Bay"

Willie Bowles

Willie Bowles, my great grandfather, joined the Irish Volunteers in 1915 soon after the funeral of O'Donovan Rossa. He bought a revolver and practiced shooting at the Hell Fire Club, near Rathfarnham. He took part in drill practice and parades, as well as other Volunteer activities. He was a member of Number 4 Section, "C" Company 4th Battalion, James's Street and Bow Lane District. He served under Captain Tom McCarthy.

On Easter Monday 1916 he was part of the garrison of about 23 Volunteers that occupied the premises of George Roe's Distillery (Malting House), Mount Brown. They barricaded Bow Lane to obstruct British reinforcements getting to the city. Willie and two other Volunteers took up positions on the middle floor of the building. The garrison held their positions for Monday and Tuesday until supplies ran low, whereupon they were ordered to abandon the premises under the cover of darkness on Tuesday night.

During the War of Independence Willie stored explosives and monitored British military activity in the city. He was also involved in raids to gain weapons. He was arrested and interned in Ballykinlar in December 1920. He died in 1964 at the age of 86. He received military honours at his funeral in Glasnevin Cemetery.

Dave Murphy
Great Grandson

Matthew Burke

Born in 1885 Matthew lived in 41 Chamber Street with his two sisters and one brother. In 1902, at the age of seventeen, he married Bridget Haydon. They had six children, but between 1906 and 1916 four of their children died.

In September 1913 Matthew was arrested for taking part in a riotous assembly in O'Connell Street. It was around this time that he joined the Irish Citizens Army (ICA). In 1916 Matthew was a member of the 4th Battalion and fought with the Marrowbone

Matthew Burke

Lane Garrison. He was arrested and taken to Richmond Barracks. From there he was sent initially to Knutsford Prison and then to Frongoch in Wales. Matthew developed rheumatic fever in prison and as a result suffered very poor health up until his death, aged 40, on 25th November 1925. His wife Bridget married for a second time. Matthew is buried in Glasnevin Cemetery along with his four children.

Matthew's brother, Edward, who lived in Meath Street, was also a member of the ICA and fought in the College of Surgeons.

Helen Burke & Liam Graham
Grandchildren

James Butler: 'Is é mo Dhaideo é'

Is é Jimmy (James) Butler mo Dhaideo. Rugadh é i Mí na Nollag 1898. Bhí sé sna Fianna Éireann ó bhí sé ina bhuachaillín óg. San daonáireamh i 1901 bhí cónaí air i mBoatman's Lane, Cé Usher i mBÁC. Bhí a athair agus a mháthair ag obair mar chúipéirí i nGuinness. Lean sé féin an ceard céanna. D'éirigh sé amach ar Luan Cásca 1916 i gCearnóg Síorghlas, Sráid Chorcaí. Ní raibh sé ach seacht mbliana déag d'aois agus bhí sé ina bhall de Chomplacht 'C' den 4ú Cathlán. D'éirigh a dheartháir ba shine Con (Christopher) amach le Complacht 'F' agus a dheirfiúr Ciss (Mary) amach mar bhall de Chumann na mBan.

Bhí Jimmy ar dualgas i nGrúdlann Watkins agus is dócha gur de bharr a óige is a bhí sé, is ag tógáil teachtaireachtaí a bhíodh sé. I litir mholta a scríobh Joe Mac Grath faoi, dúirt sé:

"Miss Cissy Butler, with some companions, was in touch with the Marrowbone Lane Garrison during Easter Week of 1916. She delivered letters at my request and co-operated with her brother Jimmy in getting information regarding the disposition of British Troops in the area. Jimmy was a member of the Garrison and, under my orders, actually mixed up with the British Forces (posing) as a street urchin, in his bare feet. He was but a boy at the time. The service rendered by his sister Cissy was very valuable. The eldest brother Con was also a member of the garrison – a crack shot and he did excellent work."

Tar éis an Éirí Amach coinníodh Jimmy i ngéibheann i mBeggars Bush. Scríobh sé litreacha uaidh sin le peann luaidhe chuig a ghrá gheal óg – Lizzy Stewart. Bhí cónaí

James Butler

uirthi in Ebeneezer Tce agus ní raibh aici ach sé bliana déag d'aois. Fíodóirí síoda a bhí ina muintir sna Tenters i mBÁC. I litir amháin (sliocht as) scríobh sé:

Well Lizzie you will be talking about writing a long letter but I don't know what to put in it as there is no Complants (sic) to make only being here for nothing. Tell my mother not to send in any more food as we get plenty of it here and the Boys are very kind to us. …Your fond lover Jimmey with love xxx.

De bharr a óige scaoileadh amach é tar éis seachtaine. Lean sé ar aghaidh agus é gníomhach sna hÓglaigh go dtí 1923. Phós sé Lizzie agus ba ise mo mhamó. Cailleadh Jimmy i 1950 agus gan aige ach 51 bliain d'aois. Bhí an galar diostróife ar an bhfear bocht. Ar dheis Dé go raibh a anam dílis, réabhlóideach, poblachtánach agus Gaelach.

Colm Ó Cinnseala
A Gharmhac

Byrne Family

George Byrne was born at Elm Park, Merrion Rd, in 1858. His parents William Burne and Louisa McElligott were Church of Ireland. George married Hester Bryan, a Catholic, in 1889. He converted and was ostracised by his family. George and Hester had eight children. In 1901, the 'Burne' family was living at Mount Anville in Co Dublin. In 1911, now known as the 'Byrne' family, they were living at The Coombe in the Liberties where Hester's sister Winifred also resided. By 1914 they lived at Susan Terrace, Donore Avenue. It is thought that their interest in the Republican movement developed through their involvement in the local branch of the Gaelic League and especially their attendance at Céilís. Five members of the Byrne family were active during Easter Week 1916 – **Winifred, May, George, William and Gerald**. A younger sister Cathleen, then aged 14, was sent home

William Byrne

Winifred Somerville (née Byrne)   *May Doyle (née Byrne)*

by Cumann na mBan. (She later married John Potts and their son Seán Potts, played with The Pipers Club and The Chieftains.)

Winifred and May were members of *Craobh Inghinidhe*, Cumann na mBan, and served at Marrowbone Lane distillery. Winifred was called home on the Wednesday of Easter week as her mother was unwell. Family lore says that she was none too pleased as she was older than May but May outranked her. May was one of the 77 women arrested and detained at Richmond Barracks and imprisoned at Kilmainham Gaol after the Rising. She was released on 8th May 1916. May was elected

George Byrne

2nd Lieutenant (in 1917), as 1st Lieutenant (in 1919), and promoted to Captain in October 1920. She resigned from the organisation in January 1922. Winifred and May later married Walter Somerville and Michael Doyle respectively. They both reared their families in Dublin.

George, William and Gerald (Garry) were all with "C" Company 4th Battalion. George served at Roe's Malting House; William and Gerald were at South Meath Bridge, Hill of Tara, and Tyrellstown House.

Born in 1891, George married Mary Dunne, whose brother Patrick J was also active during Easter Week. George worked as a wood turner with Crampton's in Ballsbridge until his retirement. He died in 1971. He was given a gun salute in Deans Grange. Family lore says that although he attended commemorations, he never spoke about the Rising.

William was a Linotype Operator. His job with the Meath Chronicle brought him to Kells where he organised the Drumbaragh/Carnaross Volunteer Company. Gerald (Garry) was dispatched from Dublin, reluctantly, to take charge of the Meath Volunteers, including his brother

William. The brothers received word around midnight on Easter Sunday that operations were cancelled. However, learning that the Rising had taken place in Dublin on the Monday, Gerald proceeded by bicycle towards Dublin. William got word on Wednesday that Gerald was at Tyrrellstown House, Dunboyne, with some Louth Men and he joined them that day. They remained at Tyrrellstown until Monday 1st May 1916.

Gerald served throughout the War of Independence. He and his father, George (Snr), were arrested on 6th December 1920. They were initially detained at Wellington Barracks (Griffith College), and then moved to Ballykinlar Internment Camp, Co Down. Soldiers called to the family home looking for Gerald and George. Gerald's father, George (Snr) said "I'm George Byrne" thus taking the place of his son, George, whose wife was expecting a baby. Gerald took the Pro-Treaty side in the Civil War. He married Emily Finlay and reared his family on Downpatrick Road. William married Mary Anne Clerkin, a Kell's woman, and reared his family at St Catherine's Avenue, South Circular Road [see P J Dunne].

Byrne Family[20]
George Byrne: Son, Nephew; Don Farrell:Nephew; & Zita Bolton-Bowes: Granddaughter and Grandniece

Gerald Byrne: photograph taken while in prison in Ballykinlar, Co. Down 1920.

John Connolly

My father, John Connolly, lived at 35 Pimlico at the time of the 1916 Rising, just a few doors up from where James Connolly lived with his wife Lily and children. He was attached to the 4th Battalion branch of Na Fianna.

My mother Elizabeth (née Gaynor) was a member of Cumann na mBan. She lived at 29 Cook Street, Dublin. Her father was an avid Republican and he eventually became the Quartermaster of "C" Company 4th Battalion Old IRA. After all the "troubles" were over my father joined the 26th Battalion of the National Army in Collins Barracks, Benburb St, close to where we lived. It is believed that my mother and father met at a meeting in that Barracks. They were married in 1924 and had a family of 5 Girls and 2 Boys. My father always sang *"Down by the Glenside"* as he polished his shoes. He received a number of medals and pensions from the Government. My mother died in April 1945 at the Hospice for the Dying in Harold's Cross. Our family was split up and we were all sent to various places around the country. Sadly, none of our surviving family has a photo of her. One little anecdote which survived in our memories was that she hid a Volunteer under her long black skirt when the 'Tans' raided her home. It is believed that during the War of Independence my father detained two British Soldiers and disarmed them in the area of Thomas St, and apprehended two men that

James Connolly on right with cousin Edward Healy on left.

had robbed a Post Office in Rathfarnham, or in Cork St Dublin. It is also said that when the 'Tans' raided his house looking for him, he threw his gun in the "slop bucket" and escaped out over the roof. My father died in 1981 and was buried with full military honours in Mount Jerome Cemetery.

James Connolly
Son

Cooney Sisters

Annie, Lily and Eileen Cooney were three extraordinary women whom history collectively remembers as "The Cooney Sisters". Aged 20, 18 and 15 respectively, during the Rising, one is struck by their political awareness despite their tender years. From a family long committed to Irish Freedom they were both courageous and principled. Educated by the Sisters of Charity, Annie trained as a Ladies Tailor in Brown Thomas, Grafton Street. Lily trained as a Developer/Printer in Lafayettes, Westmoreland Street. Eileen, the youngest, kept house for the family. Their mother was a cook in the Vice-regal Lodge, now Áras an Uachtaráin.

Having joined the *Inghinidhe na hÉireann* branch of Cumann na mBan in 1915, they were heavily involved in preparations for Easter week. The Cooney home was a centre of activity; receiving boxes of ammunition at night, distributing pikes illicitly made in Inchicore Railway Works, coordinating and delivering messages including mobilisation orders, and making signal-flags. On Easter Monday at noon, the Cooney sisters, and their Cumann na mBan colleagues, entered Marrowbone Lane Distillery with "A" Company of the 4th Battalion. They spent the week cooking as well as administering First Aid to the Garrison. Upon hearing of the surrender order, the 22 members [sic] of Cumann na mBan chose to surrender alongside the Volunteers – the only group of women to do so. They were marched as part of the garrison to Richmond Barracks where they were detained overnight with another 55 female detainees before being moved to Kilmainham Gaol. There, they were forced to listen to the executions of their friend, Con Colbert, and the other condemned men before their own eventual release. Not

The Cooney Sisters[21]: L-R: Lily, Eileen, Annie.

surprisingly these events marked them for life. Annie, as the specific recipient of Con Colbert's Rosary beads, used them in prayer all her life and taught her daughters to pray for the repose of his soul and all the brave souls who died for Ireland.

Orla McKeown
Granddaughter/Grandniece

William Corrigan

In an Irish Time article, published on 5th May 2014, Conor Gallagher wrote of the trial of an Irish solicitor which had taken place 98 years previously, in the aftermath of the Easter Rising. That solicitor was William Corrigan who:

"was born in Dublin in 1888, the son of an undertaker and Irish Parliamentary Party member, Ald. Patrick Corrigan. He attended Blackrock College where he excelled in rugby before qualifying from Trinity College as a solicitor. He immediately began work in his older brother Michael's firm on St Andrew Street, which became known as Corrigan & Corrigan."[22]

In a witness statement submitted to the Bureau of Military History, signed on 3rd May 1949, Corrigan confirmed that he:

"took part in the Insurrection being in the

William Corrigan

South Dublin Union where I was taken prisoner and after some days was brought before the court martial. Before going into the room in which the court martial took place I was seen by Mr. W.E. Wylie K.C. (afterwards Judge Wylie) who was acting as Prosecutor…We were both surprised to see each other in our respective capacities."[23]

Four years later, Corrigan and Wylie's paths crossed again but this time in very different circumstances. Corrigan recalled one particular conversation:

"towards the end of 1920….he…[Wylie]… asked me 'what are you fellows fighting for' and following a discussion about this he then said it was a pity that something could not be done to bring the two sides together. He asked me would Arthur Griffith and Michael Collins meet a British Representative. He suggested Sir John Anderson the General Permanent Secretary in Dublin Castle as the British Representative and I agreed to make some enquiries and let Mr. Wylie know the result of same. I interviewed Arthur Griffith in the Bailey Restaurant and told him of my conversation with Mr. Wylie. He stated that he would not be in favour of Michael Collins meeting any representative as his appearance was not known to the British but he thought if Collins was agreeable, he, Griffith, who was well known to the Authorities would be agreeable to meet the British Representative."[24]

Undertakings of safe conduct having been given on both sides, the meeting between Griffith and Anderson took place on 26th September 1920 in the offices of Corrigan & Corrigan Solicitors. However, William noted that:

"one took the front office and the other the back office and Mr. Wylie and myself acted as intermediaries between them. I do not think the two men actually met during the course of the proceedings but I think these were the first steps towards peace negotiations".[25]

Editors' Entry

Michael Cunningham

Michael, my maternal grandfather, was born in March 1888. He was married with two children, and worked as a silk weaver. Michael was part of the group initially assigned to Roe's Malting House; following its evacuation, he subsequently made his way to, and fought at, the South Dublin Union.

Family lore records that "when the British Army were searching and tearing up houses along Michael's street, his wife doused the front door in holy water and when the Army searched their house they were 'mute and mild'. This mildness was attributed to the effect of the holy water. Guns hidden under the floorboards were not discovered. When it became necessary to dump the rifle(s) hidden in the house, my grandmother carried them under her long skirt to the canal where she surreptitiously dumped them despite the presence of British troops.

Michael's son, my father, was a baby in his

Michael Cunningham

pram in 1918-9 when, outside the door of the house, a gunfight broke out. The family was unable to rescue the baby because of the bullets flying around until the fighting subsided. This was a very scary time for my grandmother.

Michael's brother, my granduncle Andrew, was born in December 1889. Married with two children he worked as a silk weaver. It is unclear to which Unit of the Irish Volunteers he belonged. He was shot near the Pigeon House in Ringsend and died, on 1st May 1916, aged 27.

Brian Cunningham
Grandson

William Dempsey

Born in 1893, William Dempsey was about 23 years of age at the time of the Easter Rising. In his application for a military pension, William stated that he was not mobilised on Easter Sunday 1916 but joined the Irish Volunteers later that week. He left his employment in Guinness Brewery around 1.00 pm on Wednesday, 26th April 1916 and joined the Volunteers at Marrowbone Lane. Under the command of Séamus Murphy, William served with "C" Company, 4th Battalion until the surrender on Sunday, 30th April 1916, during which time he defended the building, carried arms and repulsed enemy attacks.

Following the surrender William was imprisonedin Richmond Barracks. He was subsequently transferred to and interned in Knutsford Prison from April 1916 to his early release in June of that year. On his return to Dublin, William rejoined "C" Company and assisted in the re-organisation of the 4th Battalion. He remained on active

William Dempsey

service up to the Truce, in 1921. William died on 9th September 1963, aged about 70.

Liam Dempsey
Son

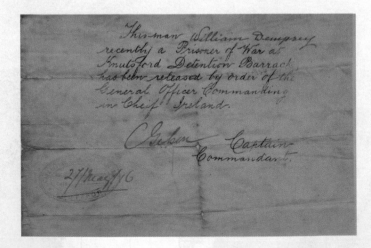

Order of Release for William Dempsey from Knutsford Prison, May 1916

Seán Dowling

My father, John Philip Bernard Dowling, was born in Cullinswood, now Ranelagh, on 29th January 1896. His father James (1856-1939) and mother Marcella (1859-1946) lived at Belgrave Road. They had nine children of whom John was the second youngest. John (Seán) was taken out of Synge Street in 1909 to join his younger brother, Frank, at St Enda's when it moved to Rathfarnham. The friendships he made at St. Enda's, together with his family background, developed his interest in Irish nationalism. The Pearses were family friends and frequent visitors. Seán joined the IRB in 1913 and subsequently the Irish Volunteers. The 4th Battalion area stretched from Kilmainham and Inchicore back eventually to Rathfarnham. Their first public display was a march to collect Mauser guns from the Asgard in 1914. The funeral of O'Donovan Rossa, 1915, was the next public sighting, supporting P.H. Pearse, who made the famous graveside oration. At the time of the Rising only about 200 took part.

Seán's first involvement in 1916 was in Roe's Malting House. That occupation lasted only a few days. On disbanding the younger members, including Seán, were allowed to go home.

Seán Dowling

Seán was later involved in the War of Independence but it was not spoken of in the household. Since, however, he was promoted to Captain and then Commandant of the 4th Battalion it can be assumed he had an involvement. Having attained an Arts degree in English and History he qualified as a dentist in 1920. He served on the IRA HQ as director of intelligence during the Civil War and subsequently spent a short time in the UK and USA before returning to Dublin. He married Joanna McCarthy (d.1955) in 1931 and they had eight children. Seán became President of the Old IRA Cumann and was involved in supporting applications for IRA pensions. He served for decades on the Kilmainham Gaol Restoration Committee, becoming Chairman and Trustee. He was also Trustee of St. Enda's. He wrote plays for the Abbey, sketches for Radio Éireann and historical theses. A keen oil painter and fisherman he played a few tunes on the piano and had a fine tenor voice.

Ó Dúnlaing family

Front page of memorial mass leaflet. Courtesy of Dowling Collection.

Peadar S. Doyle[26]

In his witness statement to the Bureau of Military History, Peadar S. Doyle wrote:

"There were many stirring events and there are many stories to be told, but I will be content to refer to the remarkable courage and daring of Captain Con Colbert, who was in full charge of the F.Coy., IV Batt throughout the whole period. Lecturing one night in Emmet Hall he warned those present who numbered about 30, that if there was anyone in their Company who was afraid to die they should make up their minds by the coming week as to their future intentions...

Doyle recalled how, on Easter Monday morning, he was:

"reading the Daily Independent at five minutes past nine precisely, when Captain Con Colbert knocked at my door and inquired for me. My wife having directed him to my room he said to me "Good morning, Peadar". "Get to Emerald Square, Dolphin's Barn by 10 o'clock act as Staff Orderly to Commandant Éamonn Ceannt"... I immediately dressed and bade what at the time I thought was a last farewell to my wife and

Peadar S. Doyle.

family. I walked by Golden Bridge Grand Canal and arrived at Emerald Square at 10 a.m. precisely, to find that I was the first to arrive excepting a Policeman on duty. I will leave it to your imagination as to how one could or should feel under the circumstances, parading for about half an hour attired in a semi-military uniform, fully armed and 500 rounds of ammunition, etc. and your only companion a Policeman. However, relief came at last by Paddy McGrath shouting through a yard gate "Come in out of that". On entering the yard there was the late Mr. John McCabe's cart loaded with war material and flying two large tri-colours. It was now nearing 11.30 and over 100 Volunteers had by this time assembled, including Éamonn Ceannt, Cathal Brugha, Liam T. Cosgrave and Con Colbert.

At this time, while the Volunteers were assembling at half a dozen centres in the City, the Citizens were bustling through the city to take the fullest advantage of enjoying themselves. It was gloriously fine and there was no thought in the ordinary mind that an insurrection was in the making. However, they had not long to wait and at or around the hour of 12 o'clock Dublin awakened and knew that there was something more than a Volunteer parade afoot."[27]

Editors' Entry

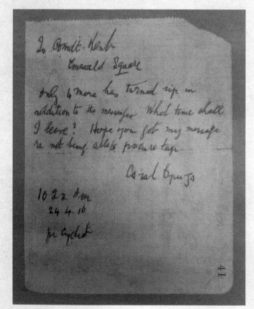

Note from Brugha to Ceannt Easter Monday 1916. Courtesy BMH CD 94/4/2.

Denis K. Dunne

My father, Denis K. Dunne, was a native of Closh, Camross, Co. Laois. He was born on the 24th January 1881. A widower in 1916, his first child had died in 1910 and his wife in 1912. He was an insurance agent with the British Legal and United Provident Assurance Company. Aged 35 in 1916, he was living in Terenure. A member of Conradh na Gaeilge and of the Irish Volunteers, Denis attended the funeral of O'Donovan Rossa in 1915. On Easter Monday, he joined his company at Larkfield and proceeded to Marrowbone Lane. Following the surrender, he was interned in Frongoch and released in July 1916.

A religious man and a Pioneer his entire life, Denis received the 1916 Medal, as well as a medal for service during the "Black and Tan" war. His activities in the latter are shrouded in some mystery but it appears that he was engaged as an Intelligence Officer in detective work. He transferred to the Citizens' Army in 1920 and ran a 'safe house' during the Civil War. He was interned for a short time. Returning to the insurance business he married Mary Kerrigan in 1921,

Denis K. Dunne

and had seven children. He was a founder member of Fianna Fáil, and served as a Peace Commissioner. Denis died in 1938.

Lorcan Dunne
Son

Patrick Joseph Dunne

Born in 1902, Patrick was 14 at the time of the Easter Rising. He lived at Hcytesbury Place, Dublin 8, and his father was a Railway Clerk.

Patrick was a member of Na Fianna, who acted as a messenger for Con Colbert. In his application for a Military Pension he later stated that he *'carried dispatches from Ardee Street to Marrowbone Lane, from Marrowbone Lane to Liberty Hall, GPO and South Dublin Union'*. Patrick served under Captains Con Colbert and Séamus Murphy, at Ardee Street and at Marrowbone Lane. He was sent home by Con Colbert as *'communications could not be established through the British Ring'*.

Patrick Joseph Dunne

However, on hearing of the surrender, Patrick returned to Marrowbone Lane and fell in behind the men. Con Colbert, once again, sent him home. Patrick was later involved in the War of Independence and Civil War. He stayed in Dublin, married Mary (May) Hitchcock, and they had had ten children, five boys and five girls, four of each survive. Dying on 11th January 1982, Patrick was buried in Glasnevin Cemetery [see Byrne Family].

Zita Bolton-Bowes
Grandniece

John Edwards

Born on 14th November 1895, John Edwards left his house at 25 St Michael's Terrace, Blackpitts, Dublin 8, on Easter Monday 1916 to fight in the Rising.

John, who was assigned to "B" Company, 4th Battalion Irish Volunteers, was employed as a cooper at the Guinness Brewery at the time. He served in Jameson Distillery, Marrowbone Lane, where his commanding officers were Con Colbert and Philip Cosgrave. At the surrender, they were brought to Bride Road and disarmed, then to Richmond Barracks. On 1st May, he was sent to Knutsford Prison and then to Frongoch, from which he was released in September 1916. John received £20 from the National Aid Fund, because of the refusal of Guinness to give him his old job back.

He rejoined the Irish Volunteers, but had to resign owing to bad health. John enlisted in the Irish Army on 15th August 1922 at Portobello Barracks and served with the Ordinance Corps at Island Bridge Barracks. He was discharged on 17th December 1923 with the rank of Private. John died on 28th January 1960.

John's brother, Michael, served with "G" Company, 1st Battalion, in the Four Courts area, King's Inns Quay, North King Street, Moore's Coach Builders, and North Brunswick Street.

Mick O'Farrell
Grandnephew

Marrowbone Lane Distillery, circa 1916. Crow's Nest is visible.

Patrick Egan:
'We are out now and we've got to see it through'

"Charles O'Grady, a companion of my school days was with me. We stuck together from our early days. When Capt. McCarthy gave the order to abandon our Post, we still elected to go it together and here we were now 'on the run'. Charlie's nerves were bad but now they were completely gone by the news we received during the day – that his elder married brother had been killed in action. Death now seemed to be right beside us. He left a young bride of about six months. I also was feeling the strain. I could not think or act coherently. I was losing all my self confidence. From the first moment I received the order for mobilsation, I immediately sprung into action. I knew what was to be done and what was expected of me. When the officers and Volunteers of the various companies stood around aimlessly at the place of assembly – Emerald Square, Cork St – it was I who took the precaution to post sentries to prevent been taken by surprise. When the captain approached me with the information of the split between Éoin MacNeill and Pearse and his followers, my reply was 'We are out now

Patrick Egan

and we've got to see it through'.[28]

Editors' Entry

The MOBILISATION ORDER FORM signed by "P. Egan" is a photocopy of the only form in existence in connection with the Easter Rising 1916. It is a historical document although the original is only a photocopy. It was displayed in the windows of the Optician and Photographer – Thomas Mason of 5 & 6 Dame Street, Dublin along with other photographs of the devastation in Dublin after the Rising. A photocopy of it is in the National Museum, 1916 Section and was also used in the film "Mise Eire" – a documentary produced for the 50th Anniversary in 1966.

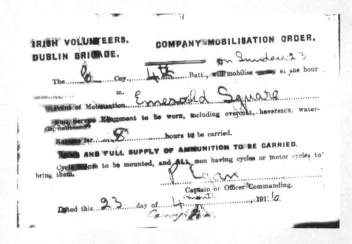

Paddy Egan was very frightened when he saw it in Mason's window. Notwithstanding, he fortunately obtained a copy but thereafter altered his handwriting to a forward slope. Family members will remember his attractive, stylish and very legible form of writing that he developed.

James Fitzpatrick: He Hoisted the Flag in 1916

With other Volunteers, James remained in Marrowbone Lane Distillery throughout Easter Week 1916. Coming under heavy fire from British forces his Commanding Officer, Séamus Murphy, once asked for *'a couple of good shots'* to counteract the attack. James volunteered and went, in his own words, *'up to the top floor. The military were firing in to the Canal. I sandbagged the window and returned the fire and kept them off '*. Amidst the gunfire of British artillery, he hoisted the Republican flag over the Distillery. He defended the stronghold until ordered to lay down arms and surrender, on 30th April 1916. James was brought to Richmond Barracks and, on 3rd May 1916 he, with 307 other prisoners, was sent first to Knutsford Prison and later to Frongoch Internment Camp in Balla, Wales until his release on 17th July 1916.

In January 1936, the Irish Press newspaper reported on the reunion of former comrades of the 4th Battalion, which took place at the Town Hall in Rathmines. The flag that flew over Marrowbone Lane Distillery in 1916, which graces the cover of this booklet, was again hoisted, this time by

James Fitzpatrick

twelve survivors from the garrison.[29] I like to think that James was among that group. My grandfather died on 7th September 1938, aged 61 years. Over 200 former comrades followed the funeral cortege, which bears testimony to the remarkable friendships forged in the heat of conflict during the series of extraordinary events that took place, on April days, in 1916.

Clare Eager
Granddaughter

Tomás Ernán Gay

My grandfather, Thomas E. Gay, joined the Irish Volunteers on 20th September 1914, the night following Redmond's speech at Woodenbridge. He was a member of "A" Company, 4th Battalion. He reported to Marrowbone Lane Distillery in Easter week and was assigned to travel between Garrisons, keeping lines of communication open and gathering intelligence. His detection of the Sherwood Foresters en route along the South Circular Road to the Distillery, and subsequent warning to Con Colbert at the garrison there, resulted in the frustration of the planned British offensive. He later carried news of the surrender from Seán MacBride in Jacob's Factory, where he

Tomás Ernán Gay

had been sent to collect supplies, to Con Colbert. Eluding capture, Gay was free to smuggle messages from prisoners and to pass on copies of the 'Gaelic American', a banned magazine, to them. He was librarian at Dublin Municipal Library and the premises were later used as 'a drop' by Michael Collins during the War of Independence. Both Collins and W.T. Cosgrave were great friends of his. Gay

became a Colonel in the Free State Army. He was married to Eileen O'Shaughnessy of Mountain View. They had three children and tragically Eileen died in childbirth, a young woman [see O'Shaughnessy Family].

Eibhlín & Tommy Doyle
Granddaughter & Grandson

John Gogan: 'A Bayonet in the Bobby's Backside'

A native of Rathgar, my father, John Gerard Gogan [1892-1944] joined the Irish Volunteers in 1915. Attached to "C" Company 4th Battalion he was ordered on Easter Monday to occupy Roe's Malting House near the South Dublin Union. He detached with another Volunteer to guard the approach at Cromwell's Quarters. Here they held up an armed policeman, later revealed to be one Constable Meegan.

Under fire from the Royal hospital they withdrew into the Malting House. On Tuesday evening, owing to a lack of food supplies and communication with the main body at the South Dublin Union, they evacuated their position. Orders were to disperse singly, leaving arms behind. John proceeded towards the North side and to his cousins in Cabra. He was arrested at John's Rd, Railway Bridge, Kilmainham. His identity was revealed when an 'Ould Wan' shouted out, *"That's the bloody rebel who stuck a bayonet in the Bobby's Backside."* The Constable in question was Meegan who identified Gogan as having prodded him with his bayonet.

After his arrest John was taken from Kilmainham Police Station to Richmond Barracks where he was court-martialed and sentenced to be shot in Kilmainham Gaol. I remember him telling us how the Gaol guards used to knock on the cell doors taunting the prisoners and calling out *"you are next"*, and of how, while waiting for their sentence to be carried out, the prisoners would say the Rosary together by knocking on the walls of their cells and keeping count

John Gogan

in time with their beads. A massive public outcry ensued following the initial executions and the remainder of the condemned – including John – had their sentences commuted to life imprisonment. John and his compatriots were shipped to Wakefield Prison and later transferred to Frongoch. Following the War of Independence, during which he was also imprisoned in Ballykinlar, Co. Down, he resumed work with the family confectionary business. He married Mary Kathleen Ryan and they had eight children. On his death a volley was fired over the grave by his former comrades of the 4th Battalion, Dublin Brigade, IRA.

Tom Gogan, Son – Australia

Robert Holland: 'We are holding the whole city'

Expressing the early sense of optimism among the Irish Volunteers, Robert Holland, based in Marrowbone Lane, later wrote that Easter Tuesday, 25th April 1916:

Robert Holland

"...broke fine and sunny, I was 19 years of age on that day, 25th April. My brother, Dan, came up to wish me a happy birthday and we wondered what part my father and my brothers, Walter and Frank, were playing and where they were. The British are now realising that it is real fight and are not leaving themselves so exposed to our fire. They formed up in Fairbrothers Field and on both sides of the canal bank and I have got up another Lee Enfield rifle. Josie O'Keeffe and Josie McGowan came along with my ration of tea and bread. Some people have evidently come in through the night or early morning with information and I hear a few more men have come in to give us a hand and that we are holding the whole city. I hear that all the country is marching on Dublin and it is only a matter of a few days until we will have the job done. All we have to do is to keep it up until they arrive".[30]

Editors' Entry

"**Walter, who was only about 15 years of age at the time, took off his celluloid collar, Captain Murphy took it and wrote a dispatch on the inside of it to be delivered to Commandant Ceannt in the South Dublin Union. I (Robert) then went back to my post and continued to fire as occasion demanded.**"

Walter Holland

Danny Raftery, Grandson

Charles Gunning

My grandfather, Charles Gunning, was a member of the Inchicore Sluagh of Fianna Éireann, having joined in 1910. During Easter Week 1916 he helped Robert Holland in the carrying of arms and ammunition from Holland's home on Inchicore Road to other locations.

Gunning was one of the boys selected by Robert Holland for the mobilisation of the 4th Battalion of the Irish Volunteers at 6 o'clock on Easter Monday morning. He also acted as a scout and messenger between Ardee Street Brewery and the South Dublin Union. Gunning delivered letters to the homes of the men in the Garrison and dispatches to the Garrison positions. Holland later recalled that it was Charles Gunning who delivered the dispatch from Con Colbert of his intended evacuation from Ardee Street Brewery.

Éamonn Gunning
Grandson

Thomas Kavanagh

Thomas Kavanagh, our grandfather, served with "F" Company 4th Battalion Dublin Brigade. He fought at Watkins Brewery and in Marrowbone Lane during the Easter Rising 1916.

Bernice Kavanagh McMaster
& Catherine Kavanagh
Granddaughters

Thomas Kavanagh

Frank Kelly

Born on or around 25th August 1895, Frank Kelly's family came from Belfast, where family history records that they were forced out from that city. Frank lived at Number 25, East Arran Street, Dublin. In 1916, he was the Quartermaster for the Company and kept the arms in his house. He was at an outpost of the Union and held the position until dark, when he retreated to The Old Men's House where he was subsequently captured. He was imprisoned in Frongoch until September 1916.

Frank rejoined the Company in 1917 and kept its arms (12 pistols). In September 1918 he finished drilling with the company in Dolphin's Barn, but was caught and arrested by the Royal Irish Constabulary (RIC). He received a 2 year sentence, reduced to 12 months. He was involved in a prison strike and riot, caught pneumonia and was hospitalised. He resumed with the company until October 1919, whereupon he then left as he needed work. He joined the Merchant

Frank and Elizabeth Kelly, Wedding Day, 31st December 1932.

navy, married and had one child, my mother. Frank died in September 1972. He disliked speaking of the Easter Rising.

Francois Pittion
Grandson

Margaret (Loo) Kennedy

A native of Donore Avenue, South Circular Road, Margaret (Loo) Kennedy joined Cumann na mBan in 1915, becoming a Captain by 1920 and Commandant by 1923. A close friend of the O'Hanlon sisters, Sheila and Mollie, she gave their niece Kate Hayes her Rosary beads on the occasion of the latter's First Holy Communion in October 1952. She died in 1953. She had remained single and lived with her three sisters.

In her Witness Satement, of January 1949, she describes her early days training with Cumann na mBan and mobilisation for the Rising:

Rosary beads given to Kate Hayes by Margaret Loo Kennedy

Margaret (Loo) Kennedy

"It was Annie Keating – now Mrs. Gerry Boland – that first introduced me to Cumann na mBan. She invited me down to 32 Lower Camden Street where the Fianna had a hall, which Cumann na mBan rented from them on Tuesday nights. We had the old Inghinidhe na hÉireann room for meetings in No. 6 Harcourt Street on Thursdays. This was in August, 1915, just after O'Donovan Rossa's funeral. In Camden Street we were trained and exercised in drill, figure marching, stretcher-drill, signalling and rifle practice with a little rook rifle. We also went on route marches regularly on our own initiative in order to train the girls in marching and in taking control. We had two instructors from the Fianna for drill, signalling and rifle practice – Séamus Pounch and a man named Devereaux (I don't know his christian name). Uniform material was available on purchase, some of us got them made and wore them. We also bought haversacks and First Aid outfits. Our branch was called the Inghinidhe ha hÉireann branch of the Cumann na mBan. In Harcourt Street we learned First Aid, Morse Code, Signalling, Dispatch Memorising, &c.

As we were the only branch on the south side we were attached to two battalions - the 3rd and 4th. On the big March Past on St. Patrick's Day, 1916, we were under orders to be ready as this might be the "real thing", meaning, of course, the Rising. We all wore full equipment and carried rations for twelve hours…

On Easter Monday morning I had a mobilisation order. I was in the 4th Battalion group, and we were mobilised for Cleaver Hall, Donore Avenue, at 10 o'clock a.m. Six or eight of us were sent to O'Hanlon's, 7 Camac Place, Dolphin's Barn, to collect stretchers, lanterns and other goods stored there. Two girls of this family were with us. When we returned to Cleaver Hall we were ordered to proceed to Emerald Square to link up with the 4th Battalion. We moved off at the rere of "A" Company in the Battalion; all the girls on parade went together to Marrowbone Lane Distillery with "A" Company, and we all remained there until the following Sunday evening".[31]

Editors' Entry

Michael J. Lynch:
'A Cup of Tea in Mrs Brannigan's Kitchen'

Following the mobilisation order on Easter Monday morning, our grandfather, Michael J. Lynch (a Volunteer in "A" Company, 4th Battalion) proceeded to Emerald Square, Dolphin's Barn, and served throughout the Easter Rising in the South Dublin Union. He later wrote that on the Thursday morning of that week:

"after having, as we thought, effectively barricaded all the windows; we were walking round, quite unconcerned. At about 6 a.m., volley fire was opened on us from the top of the Hall Range, about twenty feet higher than our building and about thirty-five yards distant. The British had been in this portion of the building since Monday.

Commandant Ceannt came across to see the place. Everything was perfectly still. There

Michael J. Lynch

was not a sound of any kind except an occasional sniper from the Royal Hospital, Kilmainham. Jim Foran and myself rambled along through the buildings and into the quarters of a Mrs. Brannigan who, with her family, had just vacated them. The kettle was steaming on the fire. There was plenty of tea, butter, bread and sugar in the cupboard, and we sat down for a good feed. We just had the tea made when we heard voices, with an English accent, and some hammering. Then an English voice said: "Go on. Put your b.... head out!" Foran and I jumped to our feet and opened the door of Mrs. Brannigan's quarters leading into the grounds, just beside the bake house. We stood very still. At the end of a small passage, between our building and the side of the bake house, a wooden partition crashed down and there slowly emerged the head of a British soldier followed by his body, carrying a rifle. Foran picked up his old R.I.C. revolver and had a quick shot. I saw the soldier pitch forward on his face. We retreated hastily into the hall and barricaded the half-glass door with a wardrobe and some furniture. We then rushed up the stairway to warn Ceannt and the other men. Were it not for that cup of tea in Mrs. Brannigan's kitchen, the British would have cut the position in half".[32]

Michael was subsequently interned in Knutsford Prison and Frongach, where his musical ability was in demand. He was Commandant of Fingal Brigade in the War of Independence but took no part in the Civil War. He died in January 1979.

Niamh & Ursula Lynch
Granddaughters

Mike Bernard McCabe

Born in 1900, Mike Bernard McCabe, my maternal uncle, lived in 3 Rutland Avenue, Dolphin's Barn Dublin. He joined Na Fianna in 1911 and later, in November 1915, the Irish Volunteers. He was a member of "C" Company, 4th Battalion. Prior to the Rising he, his brother Chris, and his father John 'The Moon' McCabe, an IRB member, were engaged in moving ammunition and pikes from various locations - St. Enda's; the Lucan Cycle Shop, Pleasant Street; Henshaws, Christchurch; Rathmines Urban District Council offices – to their house at Dolphin's Barn.

On Easter Sunday morning he left home on a horse and cart for Number 2 Dawson Street - the HQ of the Irish Volunteers - to evacuate the premises. On Easter Monday morning, following mobilisation orders he went with Captain McCarthy, – "Mike's Captain"– to Roe's Malting House. He was not engaged in any firing. His main function was signalling between the Malting House and the South Dublin Union, and in moving arms and ammunitions. He remained in the Malting House until Tuesday and then, around 5.00 p.m., he was ordered to evacuate. Along with

Mike Bernard McCabe

Volunteer P. Byrne, Mike tried to get to the South Dublin Union, James's Street, but ran into a British Army cordon at the Fountain. He went, instead, to Corcoran's of Bow Lane and stayed in that house - making several failed attempts to get out. On Saturday morning he was escorted by a Miss Lilly McLean, Cumann na mBan, to Marrowbone Lane. He remained there until the surrender, which was around 3 pm on the Sunday evening.

After the Rising he returned to school and then joined the British Army. Returning to Ireland in 1922 he took orders from Liam Mellows and occupied the Four Courts. Following the Civil War, and imprisonment, he re-joined the British Army in the Gold Coast Regiment. He also served in the Middle East and in Africa, for which he was decorated. He retired to Ireland, worked for the Rank Organisation and died, in Dublin, in 1966.

Advert for Memorial Tournament in honour of John 'The Moon' McCabe

Annie McCabe: A Widow's Plight

My grandmother Annie McCabe, wife of the aforementioned John 'The Moon' McCabe, wrote the following letter to the Ministry of Defence requesting the granting of a pension on the death of her husband. This was a long drawn out process and unfortunately she was not granted it.

3 Rutland Ave,
Dolphins's Barn
Dublin 27/6/24

Dear Sir

I desire to bring to your notice the following facts, my husband John MacCabe died on the 12th July 1917 at the Meath Hospital from pneumonia which he contracted from the results of Easter week 1916. He was a member of the IRArmy and during Easter week was carrying munitions in St Enda's to different places particularly the Distillery and the S. D Union. His horse and cart were in the Union at the close of Easter week. The cart was afterwards recovered from that place. The horse died through having been shot in the hoof and through neglect and starvation owing to the hostilities of that week and the upset of the following days. Mr E. Ceannt (RIP) who was in our house 4 Dolphin's Barn where he was residing on Easter Monday. My husband has left the following children: (10 children listed age 16-3 including twins).

The National Aid very generously made a grant of the equivalent of £600 of Corporation Stock which being transferred at the price of 60 covered about £1000. The White Cross Orphans Fund have been making an allowance for the children and I have signed an undertaking to refund the amounts so advanced out of any compensation which may be awarded me by your committee to me.

 Hoping you will give this your kind consideration
 As in the past
 I remain
 Yours truly A.McCabe.

Don Butler
Grandson & Nephew

William McDowell

William, son of Robert McDowell, was active in the Republican movement. William was married to Charlotte who was also an active Republican. By 1916, they lived with four of their children at 26 South Brown Street. William was a member of "B" Company 4th Battalion but, tragically, he was killed in action in the South Dublin Union on Easter Monday 1916.

William's brother, Patrick, fought in Boland's Mills. His name appears on the Roll of Honour for that garrison.

Pat McDowell
Grandson

William McDowell

Josephine Mary McNamara

A native of Harold's Cross, Dublin, Josephine McNamara (née O'Keeffe), was born in 1896. She was only 18 years old when, in 1914, she became a member of the *Inighinidhe* branch of Cumann na mBan, under Countess Constance Markievicz. The elder of the two, Josephine, with her younger sister Emily, was mobilised and served with the 4th Battalion in Marrowbone Lane Distillery throughout Easter Week 1916. Following the surrender, Josephine was subsequently arrested and imprisoned at Kilmainham Gaol, where she remained during the execution of the leaders. She was active again during the War of Independence with Cumann na mBan and also during the "Black and Tan" period.

In May 1966, Josephine attended the unveiling of a plaque at Galway City train station, which was being renamed in honour of Éamonn Ceannt. Sadly, following this ceremony, Josephine fell ill at the celebrations and died later the same day.

Terry Flaherty
Grandson

Josephine Mary McNamara

John Joseph Moloney: A determined Volunteer

John Joseph Moloney was 26 years old at the time of the 1916 Rising, having joined the Irish Volunteers in 1912.

Due to family illness John missed the initial mobilisation on Monday, 24th April 1916. On Easter Tuesday, 25th April, whilst the city centre was in turmoil and with hostilities in full flight, John repeatedly tried to join up with his Company, which was attached to the 2nd Battalion at Jacob's Factory. He could not gain access. Despite making numerous subsequent attempts throughout that week John could not join any of the rebel strongholds until he finally gained access to Marrowbone Lane Distillery on Friday, 28th April 1916. He proudly took up a position on behalf of the Irish Republic. Whilst John saw very limited action he was interned with his comrades in Frongoch until Christmas 1916.

Like many men of his generation, John never spoke of his Volunteer involvement.

John Joseph Moloney

His family probably never knew anything of and certainly never spoke of his experiences.

Dermot Moloney
Grandson

John Morgan

My father was born circa 1892, named John Morgan, in The Liberties, Dublin. His father was William and his mother, Bridget (née Hughes). They were from Trim, Co. Meath. They came to live at No. 10 Gray Street. His father died young. His mother took in lodgers, though the house was small. They had another son, Joseph, and a daughter, Annie (later, Annie Parker).

My father's schooling ended aged fourteen. The family was working-class, employed mostly in Guinness Brewery. The family background was Nationalist. Robert Emmet meant a lot. My father was very involved in Bulfins GAA club, based locally. It was somewhat of a Republican front. The family was Roman Catholic, but there was no sectarianism whatsoever. My father joined the Irish Volunteers (later I.R.A.). He was a member of Roe's Distillery Garrison and, then, Marrowbone Lane. They

John Morgan

assembled at Emerald Square at 11.00 a.m., on Easter Monday. They occupied S.D.U.,

Marrowbone Lane, Roe's Distillery, Watkins Brewery – the latter two were not maintained. The Countermanding Order diminished numbers but as days passed and news spread, more rallied. After the surrender he was deported from the Dublin Docks, to Knutsford Prison. He was imprisoned there and then, in Frongoch, until the final release in December, 1916. My father had some ability as a middle-distance runner, as had his brother, Joseph. While interned in Frongoch he participated in, and won races that were held for the prisoners.

My father worked in Guinness Brewery and also as a "penciller" for book-makers. He continued with the I.R.A. during the Tan War and the Civil War on the Republican side. He was interned in the Curragh, September 1922 to October 1923. Afterwards he did not get his job back in Guinness Brewery as he would not sign a loyalty pledge to Guinness Brewery for the Free State. In 1924, he went to Kerry to work for a bookmaker, for a short stay. It turned out for life, as he died in Tralee, on 11th November 1972. He spent time with Fianna Fail while there, and working as a bookie. He died without any effects. He'd speak highly of Pearse, DeValera, Brugha, Ceannt and some others.

After the Civil War, Republicans were powerless. Many went to the U.S.A. as there was little work to be had in Ireland. The country was divided, North and South.

Letter from John Morgan, Knutsford, 12th June 1916.

DeValera formed Fianna Fáil and took power in 1932 and began to flex Republican muscles. They radicalised things and diminished Britain's role in Ireland. They amended the "Treaty" agreement with Britain and began to change the twenty six counties into a Republic.

John Morgan, Son;
Emer Morgan, Granddaughter

Laurence Murtagh

My uncle, Laurence Murtagh (1881-1936), was a lieutenant in the Chapelizod and Blanchardstown section of "F" company, 4th Battalion, from 1915-16. A keen member of the Gaelic League and the GAA he helped train the volunteers at Dunboyne.

Annie O'Brien (née Cooney) notes in her witness statement that her sister, Lily, *'was sent to Larry Murtagh to mobilize the Chapelizod section of F. Company'* on Easter Monday morning. Lily went on her bicycle before she received her own mobilisation orders, which came exactly at 9am. Annie records that Lily got back in time to join her comrades in Marrowbone Lane.

Thus mobilised, Laurence, and his section of about 20 Volunteers, made their way along the canal, to join the Garrison at the South Dublin Union. They reputedly

Wolf Tone hurling club, Chapelizod. Laurence Murtagh is first person sitting on left in second row. Thomas Murtagh is second on the right in the front row.

removed their shoes in order to avoid drawing the attention of the British army as they passed Richmond Barracks. However, orders changed and they were told to go to the General Post Office instead. On arrival there, the group was halved; those with rifles were sent on to the Four Courts, as in Laurence's case, and the remainder with hand-guns stayed at the GPO. Laurence served in the Four Courts Garrison during Easter Week 1916 and was engaged in combat at Church Street Bridge. His name appears on the Roll of Honour for that Garrison.

My father Thomas Murtagh was also in the 4th Battalion but he went to Dunboyne on Easter Monday and was not engaged in action.

Vera Murtagh
Niece & Daughter

George Nolan

Born on 19th May 1901 my grandfather, George Nolan, was just 15 years of age at the time of the Easter Rising. George, from Terenure, was a regular visitor to the Plunkett family farm at Larkfield, Kimmage, where he did odd jobs. A secret IRB training camp for the Kimmage Garrison[33], it was set up by the Plunkett brothers, Joseph Mary and George Oliver. The farm was used as a clearing station for arms imported in 1914. Home-made bombs, bayonets and pikes were manufactured here.

Heavily influenced by the Plunkett family, George encountered Éamonn Ceannt, Pádraig Pearse, Seán McDermott and Cathal Brugha on their frequent visits to Larkfield. He accepted an invitation to join the 4th Battalion when approached by Harry Murray. He spent the weeks prior to April 1916 training, organising, and gathering arms and equipment.

On Easter Saturday evening, 22nd April, George was instructed to parade at 11:00 a.m. on Easter Sunday morning with "A" Company at Larkfield, in Kimmage. They assembled as instructed but after about an hour they were told to go home and hold themselves in readiness. Late on Easter

George Nolan

Sunday evening they were told to parade on Easter Monday morning at 11:00 a.m., and to bring their rifles and ammunition and as much rations as they possibly could.

They paraded as instructed and were

addressed by Captain Séamus Murphy. Informed that a Rising was to take place that day, the 4th Battalion was ordered to occupy the South Dublin Union and Marrowbone Lane Distillery. Proceeding to Marrowbone Lane Distillery, the Battalion encountered hostile civilians. They were subjected to verbal abuse as they approached the Distillery. Murphy instructed a number of groups to take control of and barricade all of the entrances and exits. George was tasked with locating, cleaning and refilling the water tanks, in case the town water supply was cut off. For the rest of the week he was posted on guard under arms and guarded the rear exits of the Distillery. On Saturday, 29th April, Con Colbert asked him to take two letters to Fathers Kieran and Eugene at Mount Argus. Colbert told him not to return to his post but to make his way home as best he could. After he had delivered the letters George made his way home, picked up his bicycle and cycled into O'Connell Street to see what had happened!

Kenneth Saunders
Grandson

Con Ó hAllmhuráin

Do réir mo chuimhne, cosúil le mórchuid daoine eile, bhí m'athair tré na cheile faoi Éiri Amach na Cásca 1916. Bhí sé i nDún Laoire maidin Luain na Cásca chéanna. Mar sin, bhí sé déanach ag teacht ar a láthair maidin Luain. Ba chóir dó a bheith suite chun ionsaí ar Caisleán Bhaile Átha Cliath. Ach faoin am sin bhí na hionsaitheoirí scapaithe. Sheol sé é féin faoi cheilt ó theach go teach gur shroich sé Lána Muire Mhaith (Marrowbone Lane), áit ar ligeadh isteach é. Chaith Con an tseachtain iomlán ann. Ní dóigh liom go ndearna sé morán ann ach, dar leis féin, d'ith sé cabáiste amh ar feadh na seachtaine!!

Bhí Con ina fhear óg, bliain is fiche d'aois ag an am. Rugadh é i gCo an Chláir agus bhí seoladh aige i gCathair Lothain taobh leis An Tullach. Bhí cruin colas aige ar Lána Muire Mhaith, mar nuair a tháinig sé go Bhaile Átha Chliath ar dúis fuair sé post ag obair i siopa grócéara i Sráid Shéamais. Ba Marcella Byrne úinéir on tsiopa chéanna. Uinhir "53" an seoladh a bhí ar an siopa.

Tar éis an Éirí Amach chaith sé tamall i mbearic Richmond ar dtúis. Ina dhiaidh sin seoladh go Sasana é, áit ar chaith sé tréimhse in Frongoch Wales agus "Wormwood Scrubs". Nuair a tháinig sé ar ais ó Shasana, chuaigh sé abhaile go dti an Clár, áit a raibh sé páirteach i mbunú an "Mid Clare Flying Column". Rugadh air níos déanaí agus

Con Ó hAllmhuráin

chaith sé bliain i mBaile Coinleora i gCo an Dún.

Tar éis an "Chonraidh" sheas sé an fód le Micheál Ó Coileáin agus bronnadh on tidéal Captaen air in Arm an Stáit. Goineadh go dona é i Léagar Luimní 1922, rud a chur deireadh lena shaol mhíleata. Fuair Con bás 1956. Suaimhneas Dé dá anam.

Séamas Greagóir Ó hAllmhuráin
A Mhac

Lily O'Brennan[34]

In a contemporary document submitted to the Bureau of Military History, Lily wrote of two incidents that occurred in Marrowbone Lane. The first tells of the fine marksmanship of the Irish Volunteers, while the second reports on rationing and obtaining food supplies.

'Fine Marksmen'

"Terrible excitement was going on outside. Already the military had attacked the Union and soon shots were fired in on us. We were divided into squads of six and I with five other girls was sent up to the storey where grain was laid out for drying... shots were penetrating everywhere and we had to move from one side to the other as the firing became intense from different quarters.

The Crow's Nest, as the best point of outlook was termed, was unprotected and our first casualty occurred here- an IV was slightly wounded on the forehead. That whole night firing never ceased and we expected an attack

Lily O'Brennan. Courtesy Irish Capuchin Provincial Archives.

all through. It was the worst night. Next day the men dug up the huge stones in the yard and carried up the earth in bags and thus protected the front out looks from the Crow's Nest. The snipers from the trees on the canal bank were easily brought down by the Volunteers- in fact the shot from the Howth gun never missed and we, who had only seen the Volunteers parading, and badly equipped, began to realise that they were fine marksmen..."

'Rationing'

"Cumann na mBan were divided in their occupations some for First Aid - cooking - washing – all prayed. The Rosary was said hourly... after the first night or two in Marrowbone Lane it was speculated that we might hold out for a month and the girls decided to leave the rations to the fighting men so that for a few days we had only dry bread and practically black tea; but from one of the bridges the word was given that 3 calves were being driven by. The gates were opened and the 3 calves commandeered. One was killed immediately and food was plentiful. Another evening a bread van was commandeered... likewise a milk van and a boy on a bicycle going with chickens and brandy to the HQ of the enemy command was held up and his goods removed"...[35]

Editors' Entry

St Patrick's Day Card sent by Lily O'Brennan to Capt. George Irvine 4th Battalion while he was in Lewes Prison, Sussex, England, 1917. ACC/2013/018, Máire Ní Dhonnchadha Collection, Military Archives.

O'Brien Brothers of the Liberties: Larry, Paddy and Dinny

I was born at No.8 Pim Street in the shadow of the Marrowbone Lane Distillery. My first recollection of those who served in the 4th Battalion was my mother (née O'Brien) recounting the exploits of her three brothers - Larry, Paddy and Dinny - who were reared at No.8. They went to James's Street CBS at the same time as W.T. Cosgrave. They were introduced to the 'cause' through membership of Conradh Na Gaeilge and Na Fianna.

Mother's accounts were mainly of their involvement in the War of Independence and the Civil War but they served with Con Colbert in the Marrowbone Lane Garrison in 1916. Larry was a Civil Servant working in Manchester who returned home to take part in the fight for freedom. A fluent Irish speaker he later became Private Secretary to Seán Lemass. Dinny and Paddy received mention in Ernie O'Malley's books *"On Another Man's Wound"* and *"The Singing Flame"*. Paddy was O/C of the Four Courts during the Civil War. He made his way to Enniscorthy (the last place of resistance) where he was mortally wounded while coming to the aid of a young volunteer. He died in Seán Lemass's arms in hospital. When he heard of the death of Paddy, Ernie O'Malley wrote that, along with the death of Cathal Brugha, it would be the end of the Civil War. Dinny, who survived, became a Detective Sergeant in the Special Branch but he was assassinated in 1942. His wife Annie

In Proud and Loving Memory
OF
Commandant Patrick O'Brien
O/C Four Courts Barracks,
WHO DIED AT ENNISCORTHY
on the 11th July, 1922.
As a result of Wounds received in Action there.
Aged 24 Years
R.I.P.
———
Ar Deis Dé go raib a anam.

Courtesy Eibhlín O'Shaughnessy Clancy.

(née Cooney), along with her sisters Eileen and Lily, were active Members of Cumann na mBan [see Cooney Sisters].

My father, Paddy Booth, married Eilish, a sister of the O'Brien brothers. He received a medal for his involvement in the War of Independence.

Tom O'Brien-Booth
Nephew

The Howth Mauser Rifle

The Ó Broin Brothers:
Pádraig, Proinsias and Séamus

Pádraig Ó Broin

Pádraig was greatly inspired by, amongst others, James Larkin and James Connolly. He was involved with the formation of the Irish Citizen Army. He fought in Marrowbone Lane in 1916; he was Section Commander. He was imprisoned and later released from Frongoch, in July 1916. With 13 others Pádraig reformed the 4th Battalion in August 1916. He married in September 1916. Pádraig became Captain of South County Dublin Company during the War of Independence. He fought on the Republican side during the Civil War. He lost his right eye in 1922 and spent 15 months in prison after the Civil War, until his release in November 1923. An accomplished poet and musician, Pádraig left a rich body of personal papers in the Military Archives. I am proud and privileged to say he was my grandfather.

Bronagh Stafford
Granddaughter

Pádraig

My paternal grandfather, Pádraig Ó Broin, lived in Rathfarnham near St. Enda's. Born in 1886, he died in 1972. Growing up, I lived around the corner from him.

Involved with various organisations

Prionsias Ó Broin (Francis Byrne)

Proinsias (Frank)

My father Francis Byrne (Proinsias Ó Broin) was born in Blackrock, Co Dublin on the 28th May 1889. His mother was Mary Tully and his father was Patrick Byrne. They

Frongoch Hotel poem from Pádraig Ó Broin collection

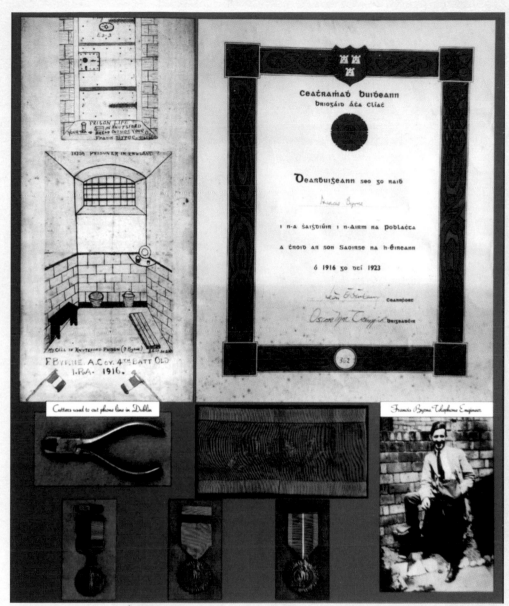

Memorabilia of Proinsias Ó Broin (Francis Byrne) showing pliers used by him to cut the telephone lines on Easter Monday 1916 in Rathmines Exchange by order of Éamonn Ceannt. Courtesy Séamus Ó Broin, son.

had five sons. He became an engineer and worked in Post and Telegraphs at the GPO from 1914, as did his brothers Pádraig and Séamus, who were a carpenter and compositor respectively.

In 1916, Francis lived at Alexander Terrace in Rathmines. On Easter Monday he reported at Larkfield, Kimmage and was asked by Éamonn Ceannt to cut the phone

lines at Rathmines Telephone Exchange, on the Upper Rathmines Road. This he did and I still have the small pliers he used. Afterwards he reported for duty at Marrowbone Lane Distillery. He remained there until the surrender on Sunday at 6 p.m. He laid his arms down on the Ross Road.

After the Rising he was sent to Knutsford Prison and on to Frongoch as were his brothers. A form in Knutsford states that in answer to questions he responded, *'I did not fire a shot. I was not fully aware of any active service'*. Finding her three sons in jail his mother wrote a letter to the Chief Secretary's Office seeking clemency or leniency for them:

"As my three boys, Patrick, Francis and James have been arrested and deported to England I beg to appeal to your sense of justice and mercy as I am a widow and now penniless having nothing but the workhouse staring at me in the face unless these boys are released soon. I know that they did not understand what they were going out for on Easter Monday…they were informed they were wanted to go for a march to Glencullen and I went to the trouble to get a lunch made up for them, along with a bottle of milk and expected them back to dinner about 6 o'clock".[36]

On his release from Frongoch, Francis was dismissed from the GPO. Having cut the telephone lines during the Rising he could have been accused of treason. His name appears on a list of staff suspected of complicity at the G.P.O, which was prepared by the Special Branch for Dublin Castle.[37] In 1922 on the founding of the Free State he got his job back. Later he became one of the first engineers to work with 2RN now RTÉ. He covered the Eucharistic congress in 1932 and was responsible for successfully establishing a broadcasting link between Ireland and Rome so that Pope Pius XII could address the Irish people. He remained with RTÉ until his retirement in 1950. He married Cecelia (Cissie) Devine and they had 4 boys and 2 girls. He died in 1972.

Séamus Ó Broin, Son

Séamus Ó Broin

Séamus (James)

Our grandfather, Séamus Ó Broin (James Byrne) was born in 1896. He lived in Terenure with his widowed mother Mary, and his four brothers. James joined the Irish Volunteers and fought with his two brothers, Patrick and Frank, with the 4th Battalion in Marrowbone Lane Distillery. He was imprisoned after the Rising in Richmond Barracks, and then in Frongoch, in Wales. James was awarded medals for his service during the Easter Rising in 1916 and later during the War of Independence.

Sadly, his wife Helena passed away at a young age, and James brought up their seven children alone. He worked in Collins Barracks after the Civil War until his retirement in the 1970s. James passed away in September 1980 and was buried with full military honours.

Audrey & Helena Byrne
Granddaughters

Re-enactment, Howth 1966. The Ó Broin brothers were present.

Hugh O'Byrne

Born in 1891, son of Hugh Byrne (master tailor) and Frances Clare (dressmaker), Hugh was a native of Harold's Cross Dublin. He joined the IRB in 1912 and attended the inaugural meeting of the Irish Volunteers in 1913. Hugh was deeply committed to the GAA; he captained the Fintan Lalor Junior and Senior teams from 1911-1923. He adopted the "O" in his surname as he became more interested in Irish nationalism. At the time of the Rising he worked as a laboratory assistant in Guinness Brewery, a position which he subsequently lost due to his Republican involvement. He was a member of "C" Company, 4th Battalion, and spent Easter Week at Marrowbone Lane Distillery under Con Colbert.

Following the Rising, Hugh was sent to Knutsford Prison and then to Frongoch where he remained until August 1916. Rejoining "C" Company, he was part of the armed guard at City Hall during the funeral of Thomas Ashe in 1917. He also guarded Ernie O'Malley in Killeen Road on the night of the latter's escape in 1920. He took the Anti-Treaty position and, following imprisonment, left the IRA. In 1923 he married Frances Cullinane with whom he had 9 children. He worked with Dublin County Council and Corporation as a

Hugh O'Byrne

Rates collector. He organised the Annual Mass and Parade for the 4th Battalion Old IRA Association at Mount Argus. He was on the Committee to have the Grand Canal Bridge at Harold's Cross successfully renamed Robert Emmet Bridge.

According to Major Val Joyce, O/C. of "C" Company, *'Hugh O'Byrne was an outstanding Volunteer who rendered meritorious service to the nation in the Volunteer movement'*. He died prematurely in 1946, having suffered unduly due to his period in prison, and while on the run.

Róisín Halligan
Granddaughter

Michael O'Callaghan

Michael O'Callaghan, my granduncle, was an Irish speaker and worked as a Coach Builder at the Inchicore Works. He was 27 years old in Easter 1916 and lived at 6 Shannon Terrace, Kilmainham. It is unclear which Company of the 4th Battalion he was assigned to but he served in Marrowbone Lane during the Easter Rising. He was sent to Richmond Barracks after the surrender and from there he was interned in Knutsford Prison in Cheshire, on 2nd May 1916, and later in Frongoch. He was released from Frongoch on 18th July 1916 [see John Traynor].

James Carberry
Grandnephew

Michael O'Callaghan

Dan O'Dowd

My father Dan O'Dowd was born on 5th March 1903. He was 13 and the family was living in Marrowbone Lane when the Easter Rising broke out. A member of Fianna Éireann under Seán MacBride, Dan began his musical career on the warpipes in the James Connolly Pipe Band, on Thomas Street. He used tell me how he was inspired by the piping of Éamonn Ceannt who played both War and Uilleann Pipes and whom he heard at the Fianna meetings.

In an interview conducted with Breandán Breathnach for Radio Éireann in 1981 in his kitchen in Donnycarney, O'Dowd[38] related that during Easter week he *'used to go up and look at the lads and talk to them in the distillery'*. He recalled the fate that met one inebriated soldier, who was on leave, and who:

"came up, drunk along Marrowbone Lane and it was like high noon in Marrowbone Lane ...I remember the soldier going up along and the women on the seats were pleading. They were all these ring women, they had their sons at the war, pleading with the soldier don't go up, Tommy, don't go up there; you'll be shot, and he was jarred and had a cane in his hand and all these squares on this shoulders...his campaign squares...and he went up and the people hung on to him and he pulled away from them going up and the next thing we heard the volley of shots and the next thing our handcart came out again and they pulled him out..."

Dan later joined the 3rd Battalion claiming that his main reason for not joining the 4th Battalion was due to his not wanting *'to be active in that area because I was blemt on anything that happened around there'*. Interned in Mountjoy Jail for his republican activities, he continued to play the pipes while incarcerated saying 'there was a big demand for me playing'. He was transferred to the Curragh Internment Camp for five months. On the day of his release, urged on by the newly released prisoners, O'Dowd related that on the train journey to Dublin:

Dan O'Dowd

"he started to play and play goodo: the train stopped and I played out and the lads helped me with me gear, me box and me few bits and things and the first one that came over to me was Madame Gonne, shook hands with me, and Miss Despard: the two of them were sitting in one of those oul trolleys with wheels on it, dressed in black and we had to shake hands with everybody and then we all got together in a ring, shook hands "anybody going my way?" A few fellows come up Bow Lane; they lived in Bow Lane. James's Street and I was on my own then home to Marrowbone Lane, me father was waiting there..."

Shortly after his release from the Curragh, while attending warpipe classes at the School of Music, the sound of the Uilleann pipes as played by Leo Rowsome attracted Dan. He became an active member in Cumann na bPíobairí from its foundation in 1936 and continued playing on the inception of Comhaltas Ceoltóirí Éireann.

Colm O'Dowd
Son

Seosamh Ó Dubhláin (Joseph Doolan)
Battle for the South Dublin Union

In his witness statement Seosamh Ó Dubhláin relates… *'My father was a Parnellite'*

"My maternal grand-uncle was a poor scholar and a Hedge schoolmaster. I was a member of the local hurling club in Offaly, where I was born, and on coming to Dublin I continued my hurling activities with one of the Dublin hurling teams (Faughs). In 1914 when the Volunteers were formed in Larkfield… I joined immediately. I was in "A" Company, 4th Battalion, of which Éamonn Ceannt was Captain…

The insurgents in the South Dublin Union were divided into two parties, one in the Night Nursing Home under the command of Ceannt and Brugha, and the other in the Board Room under the command of a Lieutenant (Ger. Murray). Some four or five men under command of a Captain [Irvine] were sent to protect and defend the rear entrance but were taken prisoners on the 24th. The enemy occupied all the remainder of the buildings, more particularly the Dining Hall, and 'twas said by some of the insurgents the church was also occupied.

There was no connection between the two insurgent forces from Monday until Thursday. On Thursday, about one o'clock, Ceannt decided to break his way through and unite the force. The British launched an attack, the most intense so far, using machine guns, rifles and hand grenades. The signal for the attack was, apparently, the blowing-in of the gable end of the Nursing Home on the ground floor from the adjoining houses with some high explosive. Having succeeded in thus making an opening, the enemy found the room into which they were rushing completely cut off with barbed wire entanglements and directly under the guns of the insurgents. The attack seemed to increase in intensity with each moment and at about 3.30 Brugha was severely wounded by a hand grenade."

The insurgent forces withdrew from the

Seosamh Ó Dubhláin

Nursing home leaving Brugha behind. The British were then observed rushing to the attack as Ó Dubhláin tells us that,

'during the whole of this attack Brugha's voice could be heard shouting above the din "Come on, you cowards, till I get one shot before I die. I am only a wounded man. Éamonn, Éamonn, come here and sing God Save Ireland before I die"…'

When Ceannt returned… he decided to lead back his men and again occupy the Nursing Home as he believed the British were not in possession. He gave as his reason for so thinking that Brugha would not be using those taunts were he actually a prisoner. On arriving in the yard of the Nursing Home, he found Brugha sitting in the yard, his back resting against the outer wall, his 'Peter the Painter' revolver to his shoulder, and watching for the first move of the enemy to enter the building. Truly it was the greatest, bravest and most inspiring incident of that glorious week. A wounded man, alone practically, holding the forces of England at bay for over an hour, taunting them with cowardice and proclaiming to them that he was only a weak and wounded man.

When Ceannt and Brugha met, a scene the most touching was enacted. The soldiers' spirit broke. Both men dropped their revolvers. Ceannt went on one knee and put his arm around Brugha. Their conversation was in Irish. What was said, only God knows.

After about a minute Ceannt arose, a tear in his eye. But again the soldier's spirit took control… As was suspect by Ceannt, the British had not taken possession of the building. He ordered that Brugha should be carried into the back room, placed his men in position, and the fight was continued until the enemy was beaten off about 7 or 8 o'clock".[39]

Sibéal Doolan
Daughter

"God Save Ireland say we proudly
God Save Ireland say we all
Whether on the scaffold high
Or the battlefield we die
O what matter when for Erin dear we fall!"

Version of words which Cathal Brugha sang according to family and eyewitness' while trying to stay alive in Nurses Building SDU, Easter Thursday, 1916. Written by TD Sullivan in 1867 it was adapted as the Fenian Movement's anthem and made famous by John McCormack on Phonograph in 1906.

Cathal Brugha

Liam Ó Flaithbheartaigh

My grandfather, Liam Ó Flaithbheartaigh, was in the South Dublin Union with Éamonn Ceannt. His brothers Martin and Séamus were also involved, as was his sister, Cissy. His background was in the GAA and the Irish language. He met my grandmother Kitty by teaching her Irish. He was not involved once released from Frongoch. He worked in Dublin Corporation as a rate collector. He had two sons; my father Séamus, born in 1920, and Kevin, who died aged 5. Liam lived originally in Hollywood, Co Wicklow, but according to his testimony he seemed to have been in South Circular Road at the time of the Rising. This is an extract from his witness statement given in 1949:

"As... [I was] ...Secretary of Craobh an Chliabhraigh, Conradh na Gaeilge... [we] provided a welcome to a big number of volunteers stationed at Larkfield (men who had returned to Ireland prior to the Easter Week Rising, 1916). These Volunteers attended the Branch's social functions each week. This same Branch (Craobh an Chliabhraigh), 25 Donore Ave., S.C.R., was in fact the meeting place for learning Irish and enjoying Irish dances for the Volunteers in Dolphin's Barn district.[40] Nearly every male member of the Branch was an active Volunteer, while many of the cailíní were in Cumann na mBan. Practically every man and boy in the Branch took part in the 1916 Rising, likewise many of the cailíní in Cumann na mBan. Two – Seán Traynor and Seán Owens – were shot dead in South Dublin Union on Easter Monday, 1916...

...On Easter Sunday night, 1916, while running a sgoruidheacht in the Cleaver Branch, 25 Donore Avenue, at 11.30 p.m., Captain Thomas McCarthy gave me an order from Commandant Éamonn Ceannt to Ciarán (Kieran) Kenny and myself to be at his house, S.C.R. Dolphin's Barn, at 6.45 a.m. on Easter Monday morning. Both of us assisted at 6 o'clock Mass in Mount Argus and arrived at Commandant Ceannt's house at 6.40 a.m.

...Commandant Ceannt had the appearance of having been up all night. After our arrival, Commandant Ceannt instructed me to write mobilisation orders for the Captains of all the Companies in the Battalion and to secure dispatch cyclists: for their delivery. Kieran Kenny contacted Seán ó Briain, 8 Dolphin's Barn, for the cyclists. The mobilisation orders were duly written and dispatched by the cyclists. At 7 a.m. Commandant Ceannt stated that he was going to a meeting in Liberty Hall and left the house. He gave me orders to carry on until his return. He returned at approximately 8.30 a.m. The fourth battalion was mobilised at Larkfield Kimmage and at Emerald Square."[41]

Emer O'Flaherty
Granddaughter

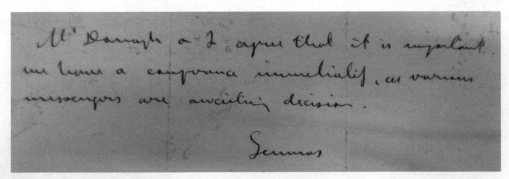

Note from James Connolly to Éamonn Ceannt, Easter Monday, 7am. Courtesy BMH CD 94/4 / 1A

The O'Flaherty Brothers:
Liam, James (Séamus) and Martin

A member of the Irish Volunteers, "B" Company 4th Battalion Dublin Brigade 1913-16, Liam O'Flaherty, along with his two brothers, James (Séamus) and Martin, were cousins of my grandfather, Martin Joseph Hodgins, of 54 Reuben Avenue, South Circular Road. As far as I know all three brothers worked at Guinness Brewery but lost their jobs after the Rising. Liam, Séamus and Martin were members of Conradh na Gaeilge.

The 4th Battalion was mobilised at Larkfield in Kimmage and the full mobilisation at Emerald Square, off Cork St. Liam left Larkfield ca. 11.30 a.m. and marched with Volunteers across Tower Field to Emerald Square. Liam was subsequently stationed around noon at McCaffrey's orchard overlooking Mount Brown to stop British military coming up from Kilmainham towards town. Liam and the other volunteers, (except Seán Owens who had been shot dead during exchanges of fire with British military), withdrew in the afternoon to the Nurses Home, and were ordered by Commandant Ceannt to take over the Hospital Ward overlooking the roadway. During the week they were based at the Nurses Home 4th Battalion HQ as an extract from his witness account tells us:

"…The Nurses Home was under fire for a whole week from the Old Men's House in Kilmainham and the back windows on the stairs were cut away by bullets. Frank Burke was shot in the throat early on Tuesday morning by a sniper in a hospital ward. He died immediately. On Tuesday evening [in South Dublin Union] at about 8 p.m., Commandant Ceannt and Cathal Brugha sent Seán Murphy and myself out by the wicket gate at rear of Nurses' Home to try and make contact with Captain Tom McCarthy's men in Roe's Distillery. Seán and myself travelled up and down Mount Brown and Cromwell's Quarters. Eventually we had the

Ó Flaithbheartaigh Crest

caretaker's house opened and we were told by the caretaker that the Volunteers had all left by that evening as they had no provisions and could not hold the building."[42]

Martin O'Flaherty is referred to in James Foran's witness statement to the Bureau of Military History. In it, Foran recalled an incident that occurred on Easter Tuesday, as Volunteers defended the front gate of the South Dublin Union:

"There was a man called Martin O'Flaherty and he said he would like to have a shot so I said to him, 'Very well, but before you have a shot at them put your hat on top of the gun and push it up easy' and while he was doing that two bullets went through it. 'Now' said I, 'If your head had been in the hat what would have happened to you?' He still has that hat".[43]

Liam O'Flaherty (Liam Ó Flaithbheartaigh) was held in Richmond Barracks immediately after the Rising where he saw Pádraig Pearse being escorted to his court martial. All three O'Flaherty brothers were imprisoned in Frongoch Camp, Wales. Afterwards Liam and Séamas remained in Dublin and Martin lived at various locations with his relatives.

Dr. Patrick Patridge
Cousin – Germany

Joseph O'Gorman

My grandfather, Joseph O'Gorman, was an Inchicore man born into a railway family, the Great Southern and Western Railway, where he worked as a foreman engineer alongside his father and brothers. As a young widower in 1913, he joined the Irish Volunteers and was attached to "F" Company, 4th Battalion. In the weeks prior to the Rising he drilled and repaired the Howth rifles in Kimmage.

Easter Week saw him waiting 'under arms' at the Cement Works, Grand Canal. On Easter Sunday he was 'standing by' moving arms, and because he had a bicycle he went with dispatches between Éamonn Ceannt and James Connolly. Dismissed at 3.00 a.m. on Easter Monday, he was roused five hours later by Con Colbert and ordered to mobilise "F" Company. He reached Emerald Square by 10.30 a.m. where the men were gathered in part uniform, with shotguns, revolvers, swords, pikes and bayonets. When that gathering moved to their posts he waited for the late-comers. They reached Marrowbone Lane at 3.00 p.m. with Moggy Keogh's horse and a cartful of weapons. The gates of the Distillery were thrown open to cheers from the inside and the men took up their positions. Joseph was described as a 'good shot' familiar in the use of Martini, Howth, and Lee Enfield rifles.

Joseph O'Gorman

Presentation of 1916 Medal to Joseph O'Gorman in 1941 by Éamon De Valera

The Garrison was dumbfounded and dejected when ordered to surrender. Con Colbert cried. At this point Joseph was injured by friendly fire. Some threw their weapons on the ground in disgust at the surrender and this may have caused his injury. How he managed to walk to St. Patrick's Park on Bride Street and then on to Richmond Barracks with a bullet in his leg is unimaginable. Joseph spent two months in the Red Cross Hospital in Dublin Castle. While there he was appointed Commandant by Cathal Brugha, over a ward of 38 soldiers. Later he was imprisoned first in Kilmainham Gaol, before been sent to Knutsford and Frongoch. On his release he re-joined his Company.

By 1918 Joseph had remarried and had a young son, whom he named Con, after Con Colbert. He tried to retrieve his position at the railway but was told that because of his part in the Rising, in spite of 25 years service, he was never to be taken back or considered for a pension.

Anne O'Gorman
Granddaughter

Charles O'Grady

My father, Charles O'Grady, first joined Fianna Éireann and later, in 1913, the Irish Volunteers. He lived in Chancery Place in 1916. He was attached to the South Dublin Union under Éamonn Ceannt and on active duty in Easter Week. He led the contingent stationed in Roe's Malting House. Charles survived; sadly my uncle, John O'Grady, was not as fortunate.

John was 26 years old, and only 9 months married, when he was killed during Easter week. He served in Jacob's Factory; on the Thursday of Easter Week he was on reconnaissance on a bicycle around Stephen's Green and was shot by British machine gun fire as he turned into York Street. John died three hours later, in the Adelaide hospital, due to internal bleeding. He was buried in a small Protestant Graveyard in James's Street to divert the attention of the British soldiers from the family as many were involved in the Rising [see Patrick Egan].

Cathal O'Grady
Son

Charles O'Grady

A member of "C" Company, Charles served first in Roe's Malting House and, after its evacuation on Tuesday evening, in Marrowbone Lane. He later recalled the events of Monday and Tuesday, 24th-25th April 1916, when the Officer-in-Charge, Captain Tom McCarthy, came to his house and ordered him, and 1st Lieutenant Pat Egan, to mobilise their half-companies, which they did. O'Grady recalled the events of Monday evening, when the Volunteers based at Roe's were:

"...constantly on the alert as we were sure the enemy would attack during the night. We had no communication with the Union and had no news of how the fighting had gone; the only enemy troops we had seen were Red Cross men and one unarmed British soldier who passed down Mount Brown. Vol. Jack Owens of B/Coy was killed in the Union field opposite our front windows. He had been firing steadily for some time and I believe he was caught by fire from the machine guns we could not locate. A Red Cross man from our Battalion, Vol. Gannon, crawled out to him and did all he could to ease his suffering but he died shortly afterwards... the men were worn out; the strain of waiting for action was telling on us all. All efforts to get in touch with the Union failed.

[Tuesday morning]... dawned over a weary garrison. We went round the men and checked up on all the posts; every man except one was there and ready to do his bit. Some time about 4o'clock on Tuesday I went down to the middle floor and found the men kneeling down saying the Rosary. When it was finished Captain McCarthy told the men he had decided to evacuate the place as he saw no sense on holding it any longer as we had no food supplies and our ammunition was so scarce. As he was our O/C and as soldiers on active service, we obeyed his order. The men were told to leave in small groups and it was every man for himself. Some of the men got down James's Street and round to Marrowbone Lane without being spotted by the enemy; others walked right into them and were taken prisoner...".[44]

Editors' Entry

James O'Hagan

I don't have a lot of information about my grandfather. He died aged 41 when my mother Margaret O'Hagan was only 6 years old. He was an only son and his family name was Hagan. As soon as possible he changed his name, putting the "O" back in to it. He worked in Guinness Brewery. James fought from 1916-1923, and was based in Roe's Malting House, Mount Brown, during Easter week. My grandmother was Julia O'Hagan (née Cullen). They had been dating but were unable to get married as a result of his involvement. Following the surrender he was sent overseas to prison. I'm not sure which prison but my grandmother was told by a fellow prisoner that he had been badly treated there and had been pulled down stone steps by his feet, which meant his head received a bang on every step. This resulted in his early death, which his death certificate states was due to 'premature dementia.'

My grandparents married and had 4 children. Sadly, my grandfather never saw them grow to adulthood. When he died Peter was 8, Margaret 6 (my mother), Sheila 4, and James, aged 2 years. All are now deceased. James was very proud that he had two sons to carry on his name but unfortunately neither married and the O'Hagan family name died with them. Only my mother and her sister, Sheila, had children.

My grandmother, Julia, received two medals in the post after his death. She placed a single Red Rose in each box with each medal. My mother, Margaret Penrose (née O'Hagan) was raised to be extremely proud of her father, and that pride has

James O'Hagan's 1916 medal

naturally passed down through the family. Both medals and roses remain in their original boxes and have been passed down in turn to my son, David Brien.

Martina Brien (née O'Hagan-Penrose)
Granddaughter

O'Hanlon Family:
Sheila, Mollie and Luke Thomas

Sheila

My Aunt, Sheila O'Hanlon, was born in 1895. She was the eldest daughter of James and Rose, 7 Camac Place, Dolphin's Barn, a home steeped in Irish history and music. The family was affected by the speeches of Patrick Pearse at the funeral of O'Donovan Rossa, and at a public meeting in Dolphin's Barn. Her father's friendship with Éamonn Ceannt was also a big influence on them.

Sheila joined Cumann Na mBan in 1915, and her commanding officer was Margaret (Loo) Kennedy, later a Senator. The women of Cumann Na mBan were vital as couriers. Apart from conveying messages they also carried small arms. A quantity of arms, first aid equipment and other provisions were stored in Sheila's home in preparation for the Rising.

On Easter Monday Sheila mobilised her squad on the orders of Éamonn Ceannt and went to Cleaver Hall and from there to Marrowbone Lane where she remained until the surrender, the news of which was greeted with shock and disbelief, reducing some of the men to tears. It was suggested the women slip away to avoid arrest but they all insisted on staying regardless of their fate. They marched out singing and were brought to Richmond Barracks and from there to Kilmainham Gaol. While there Sheila heard the volleys of shots when the first leaders were executed, a sound she never forgot.

She continued to work for Cumann Na mBan and took part in the War of Independence and the Civil War in which she took the Republican side, as did the majority of the women. She was courier to Frank Aiken (later Government Minister) who gave the order to "Dump Arms" at the end of 1923. She was one of the last women, together with Countess Constance Markievicz, to be released from the North Dublin Union in October 1923.

Sheila O'Hanlon

She met, by happy chance, Gilbert Lynch, who had come from Manchester with guns and ammunition on Good Friday 1916. He subsequently manned the barricades in North King St. They married in 1924, a wonderful couple who deeply loved each other and Ireland.

Kate Hayes
Niece

Mollie

Born in 1897, my Aunt, Mollie O'Hanlon, was the second eldest in the O'Hanlon family. Like her older sister she was a member of Cumann Na mBan. She joined the organisation in 1915 and served continually to 1923. She was a Squad Leader in the 3rd and 4th Battalions under Commandant Margaret (Loo) Kennedy. According to Patrick Flanagan, Vice-Commandant, 3rd Battalion, Dublin Brigade, Mollie was a highly efficient member of Cumann Na mBan.

She was on active service with Cumann Na mBan during Easter Week 1916. On Easter Monday she was mobilised on orders of Éamonn Ceannt to Cleaver Hall, Donore

Mollie O'Hanlon

Avenue, and from there to Marrowbone Lane Distillery. On the Thursday she was sent out by Captain Con Colbert to collect supplies from her home and the home of Éamonn Ceannt. However she found that the British military had taken control of the canal bridges and had occupied her own home. She tried to make her way back to her garrison at Marrowbone Lane but she was stopped by the British forces and ordered to turn back. The British were tightening their cordon around the distillery and all movement in and out of the area was under their control.

She was active through the War of Independence, evading arrest, carrying dispatches and weapons. Her home at Camac Place and her place of business were constantly raided. In 1917, she kept vigil outside Mountjoy Gaol during the Thomas Ashe hunger strike and was on parade at his funeral. She took the Anti-Treaty side in the Civil War.

Mollie was awarded a pension for her service to her country and she was given the 1916 Medal and the War of Independence Active Service Medal in honour of her service. She remained single and died in 1946.

Rita Tapley
Niece

Luke Thomas

My father Luke Thomas O'Hanlon (1899-1968), was the third eldest in the O'Hanlon family. Like his parents, and his older sisters Sheila and Mollie, he was actively involved in the movement for Irish Independence. He joined Fianna Éireann in 1911 and was active in that organisation up to 1923. He was a member of "B" Company (Dolphin's Barn) 4th Battalion under commanding officers Con Colbert, Séamus Pounch and Barney Mellows. He reported to Lieutenant Kevin McNamee. In the lead up to Easter 1916 the O'Hanlon family was actively involved in the preparations and organisation for the Easter Rising. The family home was buzzing with activity. On Holy Thursday Luke was mobilised for duty to bring arms from St Enda's in Rathfarnham to a safe location in Dolphin's Barn. The arms were carted by Mr. McCabe back to his home in Dolphin's Barn St.

Luke Thomas was mobilised on Easter Monday to Commandant Éamonn Ceannt's home for dispatch work. He was first dispatched to the Kimmage Garrison at Larkfield House with orders that the Garrison should proceed to the South Dublin Union. When he reported back to Commandant Ceannt's home he received orders to take food supplies from his own home at Camac Place and the Ceannt home in Dolphin's Barn to the

Luke Thomas O'Hanlon

65

Distillery at Marrowbone Lane. Most of Monday and Tuesday of Easter week was spent on this activity. Throughout Easter week he was on outpost duty, collecting arms, scouting, reporting on British troop movements in the area, and carrying dispatches. He scouted for Captain Colbert for his retreat from Watkins Brewery to the Distillery at Marrowbone Lane.

During the War of Independence his home at Camac Place was raided by the British army during the general roundup after the events of Bloody Sunday, 21st November 1920. Luke and his father were arrested and taken from the house under armed guard to Arbour Hill military prison. They were released at the end of March 1921.

He was arrested again in 1922 after the outbreak of the Civil War and he spent 15 months in Gormanstown military prison. His active involvement in Fianna Éireann more or less ceased after his release from Gormanstown military prison at the end of the Civil War. Luke was very proud of his

Fianna Éireann registration certificate for Luke O'Hanlon. PJ Young's signature is on it. (see Young Brothers)

friends and comrades in Fianna Éireann and never considered his deprivation of freedom as a sacrifice. His favourite songs were; *Wrap the Green Flag around me Boys* and *The Felons of Our Land*, which he loved to sing. One of his sayings was 'we got too little too late from the Crown'. He was proud to be able to say that he and his father met the headmaster at Saint Enda's in Rathfarnham, Commandant General PH Pearse.

Louis O'Hanlon
Son

Edward O'Neill

My great-grandfather Edward O'Neill was a member of the IRB and of "F" Company 4th Battalion, Dublin Brigade. He fought with the Marrowbone Lane Garrison under Con Colbert and Séamus Murphy in 1916. He later took part in various engagements during the War of Independence. As one of Michael Collins's staff he carried confidential dispatches from IRA headquarters in Dublin to various parts of the country. He served terms of imprisonment in Frongoch, Knutsford and in Kilmainham Gaol.

Joanne Banks
Great-Granddaughter

Edward O'Neill

Joseph O'Neill

Joseph was born in 1898, and worked all of his life in a little boot menders shop in 95 Cork Street. Aged 17, he joined "C" Company, 4th Battalion in 1915. He mobilised at Emerald Square on Easter Monday and went into Marrowbone Lane Distillery. Joseph later recalled that on Sunday, 30th April, he did not surrender with the rest of the Battalion but instead he had seen *'Mr. McGrath going out over the wall and I had heard that we were all going to get away. I followed them and got away over the back wall, into Cork Street. I left my arms behind me'*.[45]

He rejoined in 1917. Family lore recalls that in 1920 he was sent a pair of shoes from Brixton Prison, by a Mr. McGrath, for repair. He found a plan for an escape in the shoes, which Joe McGrath later confirmed was given to General Michael Collins and was acted upon.[46] Joseph married Bridget Morris in 1924; they had seven children and lived in Crumlin.

I was a young adult in 1972 when my grandfather died, aged 74 years old. All we had ever been told was that Joseph had

Joseph O'Neill

taken part in the 1916 Easter Rising. He never spoke of it to us.

Maureen Bourke
Granddaughter

Michael O'Riordan

My granduncle, Michael O'Riordan, served with "F" Company, 4th Battalion, in the Marrowbone Lane Garrison.

Louise West
Grandniece

Sketch of Michael O'Riordan by Louise West.

The O'Shaughnessy Family of Mountain View, Grand Canal Harbour

The Ua Seachnasaigh are one of the ancient Gaelic clans of Galway who were dispossessed by Cromwell in the 17th century. My grandfather John O'Shaughnessy (1853-1923) was born and raised on a farm in Athboy, Co. Meath. A committed IRB man he came to Dublin as a young man and married Mary Bergin. A native of Thomas Street, Mary was of French Huguenot origin. John O'Shaughnessy was a cousin of the Gaelic scholar, An tAthair Eoghan Ó Gramhnaigh, also from Athboy, who was first Professor of Irish in St Patrick's College Maynooth and a founding member of *Conradh na Gaeilge*. The O'Shaughnessy family lived at Mountain View, Grand Canal Harbour, Dublin, which was of strategic importance to the Volunteers during Easter week. The British army took it over for several days.

John and Mary had a family of seven children: Jane, Eileen, Eddie, Seán, Mary, Anne, and Theo, my father, who was their youngest child. Born in June 1898 his father John – then Secretary of the 1798 centenary committee – honoured Wolfe Tone by naming him Theobald Wolfe Tone. Theo and Seán were members of the 4th Battalion. Mary was in Inghinidhe na hÉireann and Jane taught with Sinéad Flanagan (later Bean de Valera).

On Easter Monday my father, Theo, returned with his sister Eileen and her fiancé Tommy Gay, (also in the 4th Batt.) from Fairyhouse and reported for duty at Marrowbone Lane. He was 17 years old at the time. He often spoke of how kind Con Colbert was to the younger Volunteers. Seán was based in the South Dublin Union where he was shot in the foot. His brother, Eddie, arranged a daring and successful escape for him. Eddie worked in the postal service and did a lot behind the scenes to help Ireland's cause.

Following the Rising Theo was sent home from Richmond Barracks because he was under 18. He and his siblings took part in the War of Independence and during the Civil

Theo O'Shaughnessy, taken in 1938.

War they were against the Treaty. He met my mother Kathleen Ryan from Dublin's north-side in the Phoenix Park where he played hurling for Crokes and she played Camogie for the Civil Service and Dublin teams. I am proud to be an O'Shaughnessy and I am especially proud of my father, Theo. He was kind and gentle and had a special affinity with nature. He had a great sense of humour and enjoyed composing comic verse. Being part of the 1916 Relatives Association has been a wonderful experience. I feel honoured to have met so many of the descendants of our 1916 heroes and heroines. *Solas na bhflaithis dár Sinsir*.

Eibhlín O'Shaughnessy Clancy
Daughter

'At Grandma's house'

Mountain View – my Grandma's house where I was reared – was occupied by the British Army in Easter Week 1916. A Captain Fisher was in command. He apologised to her, saying *'We've no quarrel with the Irish'*. He thought that he was being sent to France and felt lost in Ireland. During the week he was shot dead at the gate, which horrified Grandma. She always spoke well of him and she described him as a gentleman. Later she brought his gun down to the Distillery. Uncle Jack (Seán O'Shaughnessy) was shot in the foot in combat at the South Dublin Union. Uncle Eddie worked for the Post Office and had a Post Office Pass so he could go through the British Army checkpoints. He was able to go into the South Dublin Union, get Jack, and then come through the checkpoints by showing his card. He went in wearing two suits, one over the other so that he could give Jack a change of clothes. Returning home through the checkpoints he said that he was bringing his sick brother home from hospital. Grandma put Jack in the bed in the kitchen but then the house was taken over by the British army. Grandma told the British army that her son had the flu and that he couldn't be taken out of the bed. Uncle Jack stayed in the bed while the British occupied the house. He was later transferred to Tommy Gay's house on the South Circular Road, where he was nursed by Tommy's fiancée, Eileen O'Shaughnessy, Jack's sister. They were my mother and father [see Tomás Earnan Gay].

Mary Gay Smith
Niece

'A Miraculous Escape'

I remember as a child hearing that the man positioned on either side of my granduncle, Seán O'Shaughnessy, had been shot dead during the action in Easter week and that he had been injured and was lucky to be alive. I always imagined the action had occurred at a window or even on the stairs at the Nurses Building, when the British exploded grenades which so brutally injured Cathal Brugha. (The latter was always spoken of with great admiration by my grandparents). Then I read Patrick Egan's account of the action on Easter Monday in McCaffrey's orchard, SDU, which over-looked Mount Brown:

*May O'Shaughnessy Cumann na mBan Brooch
(courtesy Martine Smith)*

4th Battalion Army Council – After 1916: Seán Ó Shaughnessy seated extreme right, Sean Dowling seated centre. Courtesy Ó Dúlaing family.

"The firing had become intense, and came mostly from the enemy at the end of Mount Brown or Kilmainham direction…on looking out of the window, here I saw three Volunteers lying in a group under the hedge across the road. They were Seán O'Shaughnessy, George Owens and Gannon (a Red Cross man). Two were lying face down, while Owens was on his back. He was wounded and was making great efforts with his right hand to move his water-bottle to his mouth… he was slowly dying. By this time, the enemy machine guns had come into action and were whipping the hedge and field. A fourth man (McDowell?) lay on his back, with his knee up and arms outstretched, near the Union wall; he was dead. The sight was depressing; their position was hopeless – no back or cover to protect them…

…On returning to the front, we saw the Corporation ambulance come up the hill and stop on the opposite side of the road. Volunteer Owens was lifted down from under the hedge and placed on a stretcher and put into the ambulance… They did not attempt to stir the other two men. I thought they were dead, they lay so still'.

…'That morning [Easter Tuesday]… someone drew my attention to the fact that the two men under the hedge on the opposite side of the road were gone. They apparently moved under the cover of darkness during the night. (Long afterwards I learned that Seán O'Shaughnessy had been wounded in the leg and was helped by Gannon through the Union grounds."[47]

Pádraigín Ní Sheachnasaigh Clancy
Grandniece

John (Seán) Owens

My uncle, John (Seán) Owens, was a member of the 4th Battalion Dublin Brigade. He was killed on Easter Monday 24th April 1916 at the South Dublin Union and is buried at the rear of the HSE Headquarters (Dr. Steevens' Hospital) together with volunteer Peter Wilson, Fingal Brigade.

Thomas Owens
Nephew

Seán Owens

Joseph ("Joe") Parker (Seosamh Parcéir)

Joe Parker was from the Liberties and lived at 44 Reuben Street. He worked in Guinness Brewery. Joe did not like speaking of his involvement in the Volunteers at Marrowbone Lane. He would only say that he spent the week on the roof, wrapped in a blanket. When the order to surrender came, Joe was not near the others so he just "walked out" a different gate. According to Joe it seemed senseless to him not to do so. He and his friend John Keyes (of Keyes Tobacconists on Thomas St) crossed a neighbouring farm and made their way home via *"The Back of the Pipes"*.

In the immediate aftermath of the Rising, Joe quietly resumed his job in the Brewery. Family lore says that this was when the Brewery re-opened after Easter Week. Joe said nothing to his employers about what he had been up to in the previous week and his employers said nothing to him. His absence may not have been noticed and therefore, unlike other Volunteers working at Guinness Brewery, he kept his job. Joe's active involvement ended at this point.

Joe married Annie Morgan, 10 Gray Street, the Liberties, in 1924 and continued working in Guinness Brewery until his death in 1952. They remained in the area,

Joe Parker

setting up home in Mountshannon Road and later moving to 109 South Circular Rd (renumbered 521). Joe and Annie had 7 children, of whom 5 survived to adulthood.

Joe's brother-in-law was with him in Marrowbone Lane [see John Morgan].

Pauline Sheerin
Daughter

Arthur Power

My granddad, Arthur Power, was not a signatory, nor a poet or teacher but a labourer. Prior to the Rising, as a young man – only a kid – he took part in attacks on barracks in Palmerstown and Ballyfermot. He was 19 years of age when he left his house with his two brothers, Liam and Joseph, after Volunteer Robert Holland called for them on Easter Monday 1916. Arthur served in Marrowbone Lane Garrison during the Rising. Holland described him as a *'steady and reliable volunteer, always ready for duty'*.

Arthur had continuous service from 1913,

7th Coy, 4th Batt. Bluebell Cemetry after 1916. Chair left empty for Con Colbert. Arthur Power seated front row, third left, his two brothers and their father are also present.

through 1916, the War of Independence and eventually joined the newly formed Free State Army.

Brian Power
Grandson

James and Thomas Quinn:
Father and Son – 'Two Heroic Men'

My great-grandfather, James Quinn, of 2 Hammond Street, Blackpitts, Dublin, died on Easter Monday 24th April 1916. In fact, he was one of the first Volunteers to be shot and killed. His name is on the Roll of Honour at the Republican Plot at Glasnevin Cemetery and at Arbour Hill.

James was a member of the Columcille Hurling Club and reputedly he used to say that he would only exchange his *camán* for a rifle. A painter by trade, he was aged 54, married with a wife and five children, when he was killed while holding the back entrance of the South Dublin Union, on 24th April 1916. His son, my grandfather, Thomas Quinn, was fighting in Paris at the time of his father's death and unfortunately he, too, died in battle in 1917 and is buried in France.

My family has always known that our grandfather Thomas had died in World War One but knew nothing of our great-grandfather dying in 1916 until recent years. As a family, we are very proud of them

James Quinn

both. May they Rest in Peace.

Maria Brunton
Great Granddaughter

Michael Sweeney

Michael Sweeney was born 18th December 1900. Residing at 5 Harold's Cross Rd, he joined the Irish Volunteers in 1913, and trained in military manoeuvres at the disused brickworks at Mount Argus, and at Dolphin's Barn. Aged just 15 at the time of fighting, he was described as *'a brave and fearless soldier who narrowly escaped death in the Dublin Union in 1916'*. He was captured on Easter Monday and was held at Richmond Barracks and Kilmainham Gaol before being interned at Wakefield detention barracks.

Michael went on to play an integral role in the War of Independence and became section commander of the 4th Battalion, as a member of the Active Service Unit. He led the ambush at the Halfway House pub (then Yeates public house) in May 1921, considered one of the most successful

Michael Sweeney

ambushes of the conflict, in which he was badly injured. Having taken the Anti-Treaty side, Michael was shot dead by a Free State soldier while under escort from Beggar's Bush Barracks to Mountjoy. He was lame and on hunger strike at the time, on 10th April 1922. The inquest into his death, attended by the Lord Mayor Helena Molony, ruled it accidental. Harry Boland proclaimed it murder in the Dáil but was forced to retract it. His funeral from Mount Argus to the Republican plot in Glasnevin was lined by all units of the Dublin Brigade, Cumann Na mBan and Na Fianna Éireann. The AGM of the GAA at the Gresham Hotel was suspended as the cortege passed so they could pay their respects. Thousands lined the route. After the farewell volley in Glasnevin the priest, Father Joseph, said he was *'truly a martyr for Ireland as Patrick Pearse or Terence MacSwiney'*.

Mark Jenkins
Great Grandnephew

LARGE ATTENDANCE AT FUNERAL IN DUBLIN.

The funeral of the late Lieut. Michael Sweeney, who was mortally wounded in Grafton street last week, took place from Mount Argus yesterday after 11 o'clock Mass. The cortege, which comprised the units of the Dublin Brigade, I.R.A., the Cumann na mBan and Fianna Éireann, was of large dimensions. The attendance included Messrs. James O'Dwyer, T.D.; John O'Mahony, T.D.; Liam Mellowes, T.D.; Roderick O'Connor, T.D., Charles Burgess, T.D.

The procession traversed the principal streets of the city to Glasnevin Cemetery, where the remains were interred in the Republican plot. As the cortege passed Leonard's corner the Tricolour was displayed at half-mast from Wellington barracks, recently handed over to the I.R.A. The remains were received at Glasnevin by Rev. Father Fitzgibbon, who recited the prayers at the graveside.

After Last Post was sounded, and a farewell volley discharged over the grave, an oration was delivered by Father Joseph, O.P., Mount Argus. Michael Sweeney he said, was a brave and fearless soldier who narrowly escaped death in the Dublin Union in 1916, and in one of the most daring and effective ambushes that had been carried out during the closing days of the struggle. Whether his death was caused by wounds accidently received, or by the bullet of an assassin or of an honourable foe, he was as truly a martyr for Ireland as Patrick Pearse or Terence MacSwiney.

Mr. Oscar Traynor said it was unfortunate that Lieut. Sweeney's death was accidentally caused by the bullet of a comrade, but for that comrade they entertained no hatred or spirit of revenge. They would indeed, welcome him back to their ranks to help to achieve the freedom for which Michael Sweeney fought all his life.

Michael Sweeney, Obituary Notice

John Traynor: 'Only 200 yards from home'

On Easter Monday John Traynor, our granduncle, fell in at Emerald Square and made his way to the South Dublin Union. He was 17½ and reputedly told his mother he was going to a football match. He was part of Captain George Irvine's small group of seven who were assigned by Éamonn Ceannt to guard the back gate of the Union at Rialto Bridge. From here they were ordered to watch the South Circular Road and Richmond Barracks. This long wide road was a marching route for the British and holding this position was essential to inhibit British troop movement. The British did not use back lanes as they could get lost and disorientated. That morning there were 360 British troops stationed in Richmond Barracks. The Volunteers took up positions in wooden and tin outbuildings and as a result were extremely vulnerable. They opened fire on a large body of British troops, initially repelling them, until the British regrouped and returned heavy fire aided by a machine gun placed on the roof of the Royal Hospital to the north. Caught in deadly cross-fire from three directions the Volunteers were heavily outnumbered and fought bravely.

John Traynor

According to witness statements John was shot through the chest by random fire which peppered through the shed as he and Volunteer Captain James Burke were moving from one room to another. For a moment all seven Volunteers, including Irvine, [who was a Protestant], gathered around John to help and join with him as he tried to say his last prayer. Captain Irvine later said that he was right next to John when he fell mortally wounded. John was only 200 yards from his house and his mother and family could hear the shots ring out from their front room, not knowing what was going on. As the day unfolded the Volunteers fought on but were surrounded. They reluctantly surrendered as the British threatened to throw hand grenades if any more resistance was expressed. The Volunteers were taken to Kilmainham Police Station and on to Richmond Barracks. The British Military did not come out of the fight unscathed as, amongst others, they lost two officers, Captain Alfred Warmington[48] and Lieutenant Alan Ramsey[49] (see Michael O'Callaghan).

James Carberry, Grandnephew
Andrea Traynor Kavanagh, Grandniece

John Traynor medals

Thomas Venables

Born in 1892, Thomas Venables was 24 in 1916. He was a silk weaver by trade. I have no details as to how he became involved with the Republican Movement but I do know that although he fought with "C" Company, 4th Battalion in Marrowbone Lane for the duration of Easter Week, he was attached to "C" Company, 3rd Battalion prior to the Rising and rejoined that Battalion following his release from Frongoch.

My mother remembers her mother and older brothers recounting how the flag that flew over Marrowbone Lane was in my grandfather's possession after the Rising.

On release from Frongoch, Thomas played an active part in the War of Independence, including being part of the GHQ operation on 28 Pembroke Street on Bloody Sunday on 21st November 1920. He fought on the Anti-Treaty side during the Civil War. He married Annie Butler in August 1926 and they had eight children. A

Thomas Venables

deeply religious man, Thomas died on 23rd March 1955.

Suzanne Rowe
Granddaughter

Michael Whelan

Born in Dublin on 10th March 1891, my grandfather, Michael Whelan, was a Wicker and Cane Chairmaker and later taught cane making to the blind, in Rathmines. Michael joined the Irish Volunteers on 6th April 1916 and was a member of "C" Company 4th Battalion. He was living at 7 Emerald Square, Dolphins Barn in 1916. This was the 4th Battalion assembly point and as a result he was on constant alert. He mobilised at 4pm on Easter Sunday but the order was cancelled. On Easter Monday he mobilised at 10 am and, following assembly, he and 50 other Volunteers marched to McCabe's Yard, Dolphin's Barn, where he obtained a shotgun and 40 rounds of ammunition. Easter Monday afternoon he marched to the Distillery in Marrowbone Lane where he occupied a post throughout the week.

Michael Whelan

The first night at Marrowbone Lane he was upstairs on watch with a shotgun; later he moved to the carpentry workshop, and then acted as a guard at the back gate. On Friday morning he moved to guard duty on the front gate and remained there until the surrender on Sunday evening. He was deported to Knutsford Prison and then to Frongoch and released on 1st August 1916.

Michael rejoined the Company after its re-organisation, in June 1917. He continued training and drilling until the Spring of 1920 when he became ill and was put on inactive duty. He went to Glasgow to avoid capture and remained there from November 1920 until August 1921. He died on 3rd February 1967 and is buried in Mount Jerome, Dublin.

Paula Rooney
Granddaughter

Richard Whelan

A native of Avoca, Co. Wicklow, my granduncle, Richard Whelan, was born on 7th December 1895, son of Moses Whelan (a railway worker) and Brigid Whelan (née Byrne). In 1913 Richard obtained employment as a clerk in the Dublin & Great Eastern Railway Company. He took up lodgings in Rialto and became a member of the Geraldine Gaelic Football Club and Conradh na Gaeilge. He joined the Irish Volunteers in Dublin in 1914 and became a member of "B" Company, 4th Battalion.

From 6.00am on Easter Monday 1916, on instructions by messenger from Commandant Ceannt, ten cyclists – including Richard – were summoned to bring the mobilisation orders to the officers and men of the 4th Battalion. In his witness statement, his fellow Volunteer Gerald Doyle recalled:

"At 9.30am on Easter Monday morning, Richard Whelan, Company Organiser, called to my house with instructions to parade at Larkfield at 10 o'clock. I immediately contacted John Traynor at Kilmainham and proceeded from Kilmainham to Larkfield and on our way across to Larkfield we called at Whelan's lodgings and then all three of us proceeded to Larkfield."[50]

Richard was stationed at South Dublin Union throughout the week and surrendered with Éamonn Ceannt on Sunday evening. He was held in Richmond Barracks before transportation to Britain where he was imprisoned in Knutsford Prison and subsequently in Frongoch, until July 1916. On his release he returned to

Richard Whelan

Wexford and became involved in the War of Independence. General Éoin O'Duffy later called him *'a sterling soldier.'*

Richard married Kathleen Moran in Ferns in 1923. Kathleen had been a member of Cumann na mBan and had also participated in the Easter Rising at the Athenaeum in Enniscorthy. Richard died in July 1955 and was buried in Enniscorthy.

Des Furlong
Grandnephew

The Young Brothers – Éamonn Young

The son of Irish emigrants, my father, Éamonn Young, was born in Liverpool in 1900. One of ten children he came from a patriotic family. He and his siblings would get a hiding each Friday in school in England for refusing to sing 'God Save the King'. His father would say *'well, it will make Irish men out of you'*. The family returned to live in Hamilton Street, Donore Avenue, South Circular road in 1914. When he was 16 my father and his brothers Robert (18) and Tom (20) became involved in the Volunteers. He joined the 4th Battalion at the South Dublin Union. He was used as a runner. Although he hadn't an English accent he could imitate one and he was used for gaining information from the British army. He did not talk about it a lot except when we were doing history in Primary school. Once you came to 1916, he kind of filled you in on little bits.

Éamonn Young

Both before and after the Rising the house would be raided. My great-grandfather had a trunk at the top of the stairs. His name was Robert Afton and he was involved in shipping. Being smart the lads got a poker and in front of his initials 'RA' they put an ' I '. Whenever the house was raided the British army would see this trunk and go to open it. Of course there was nothing in it. While the British were attending to the trunk, it gave my Dad and his brothers a chance to escape out the back. So it was a decoy.

Following the surrender Éamonn was imprisoned in Keogh Barracks in Inchicore for eight months. He used to tell us that the room was very small. He used compare it to our bathroom at home. Twelve of them were in that room. They weren't allowed out to wash, to exercise – nothing.

On the night of his release the curfew in the city was 9p.m. He was released at 8.40pm and he had 20 minutes to run the otherwise 45-minute walk home. If you were caught out past curfew you would be locked up again- they were trying to catch the boys out. He arrived home exhausted. He knocked at the door and my grandfather told him to go around the back and take off his clothes. He came out with buckets of cold water and threw it over him to remove the filth from him.

My father used say some were never the same again when they came out. His brothers Tom and Robert suffered a lot. They spent 18 months in jail in Wales. Each was told the other was dead. They met on the altar as altar boys the morning of their release. A priest had selected the 'Youngs' to bring them together.

Dad and his brothers were active in the Civil War, choosing the Pro-Treaty side. Later he joined the Irish army and retired as a Captain. He died in 1962. Many people came to pay their respects at his funeral, including his Godson, Cathal, known to the rest of the nation as Charlie Haughey. The families had once lived beside each other in Castlebar. Despite different politics Mrs Haughey and Mrs Young remained friends for life.[51]

Catherine Moran
Daughter

Patrick John Young

My Dad's name was Patrick John Young. He was the fourth of ten children; seven boys and three girls. His father and mother were both from Dublin and for a time they lived and earned a living in England and Scotland. Dad was born in Chester in England on 31st December 1900. His parents returned to Ireland in 1910 and resided at 37 Hamilton Street off Donore Avenue. Dad's early schooling was in England and then at Black Pitts National School in the Liberties.

He joined Fianna Éireann in 1915 when he was 14 years old. He and his older brothers, Robert, Thomas and Éamonn, were members of the 4th Fianna Battalion Dublin Brigade attached to Watkins Brewery and Marrowbone Lane, under the command of Captain Con Colbert. Part of Dad's duties was to deliver dispatches to Liberty Hall and the GPO. When the surrender came he was able to slip away but his brothers were imprisoned in Frongoch. When the 4th Fianna reformed in 1917 they all became active again.

In 1920 Dad was arrested when his employer turned him over to the authorities. While he was in Dublin Castle awaiting transport to Ballykinlar, Co Down, he went

Patrick John Young

back into his cell to collect his hat. Dick McKee gave his hat to Dad saying *'take mine I won't be needing it any more'!* Dick was later killed, along with Peadar Clancy, by the British on Bloody Sunday, 21st November 1920. While in Ballykinlar Dad met Martin Walton (later of Walton's Music) who formed an orchestra, which Dad joined. He learned how to play the violin and read music. After the Truce, Dad took the Pro-Treaty side and joined Óglaigh na hÉireann but resigned in August 1923 to take up employment in the new Garda band in the Phoenix Park.

Dad attended the IRA commemorative masses all over the city accompanied by my sister Cathleen, or me. The old IRA literary and debating society was a large part of his life until it ceased operating. Dad also kept in touch with Martin Walton, making and repairing instruments, including brass moulding. Following in his father's footsteps, he worked for Ben Wafer in Hanover Lane.

A regular attendee at Mass and a Pioneer all his life he was a member of the 3rd Order of St Francis until he died in May 1990. Dad was really a fine man God Bless Him.

Patrick John Young Jnr
Son

Banner of Na Fianna, 'An Gal Gréine' showing Sunburst with traditional Pike. It is embroidered in gold thread with ancient Fianna Motto 'Glaine r gcroí, Neart r ngag, Agus beart de rir r mbríathar'. [Purity in our hearts, Strength in our limbs, and Action according to our word]. The Flag was stolen from the home of Countess Markievicz by the British army during 1916. It is displayed in London's Imperial War Museum and is currently on loan to Dublin City Council and the Irish People for 2016.

Thomas Young
'Two Amusing Incidents – Marrowbone Lane'

Inside Marrowbone Lane, circa 1916. Courtesy Jameson's Distillery website.

Thomas Young acted as a scout at Wellington Barracks, taking up a position there on Easter Monday, 1916 before moving to Marrowbone Lane. He also led a patrol to scout Watkins Brewery all on the orders of Con Colbert. He recalled two amusing incidents that occurred at Marrowbone Lane during the Easter Rising. He wrote:

"I arranged a system of signals with Sergeant Ned Neill, also of F. Company, who was in charge of the main gate. These signals would indicate to him the type of person wishing to enter, the movements of animals, vehicles and suchlike, the reason being that it was considered unsafe to open the gates without prior knowledge of the person seeking admission, and it was a means of diverting foodstuffs which might be en route to other British garrisons, the Vice-Regal Lodge and suchlike places.

As a result of this signaling system, I would like to record two amusing incidents. I signaled that there were three cattle being driven along Marrowbone Lane towards Cork Street. Ned Neill opened the gates and drove the cattle through them. He closed the gates. In a few moments the owner of the cattle came along and stood in consternation.

I asked him what his trouble was, and he replied by asking me had I seen three heifers. I, of course, assured him that no cattle had passed that way. My reason for signaling the arrival was due to the fact that, earlier in the day, a herd of cattle had passed by, the drovers, in their usual way, making plenty of noise. Captain Séumas Murphy sent for me and asked what was the cause of the commotion.[?] I replied that it was merely a herd of cattle being driven along the lane. He appeared to be annoyed at my reply and asked me where did I expect to get meat for the troops in Marrowbone Lane [?].

Another incident was when I saw a messenger boy peering through the closed gates. I noticed a basket on his bicycle containing trussed chickens, and frantically signaled Ned Neill, who opened the small wicket gate and asked the boy what he was doing and where he was going. The boy replied that he was delivering these chickens to the Vice-Regal Lodge. Ned Neill took the basket of chickens off the bicycle and told the boy to give the Lord Lieutenant, Ned Neill's compliments. The boy's reply was; "For…sake, Mister, take the… bicycle as well…" [52]

Editors' Entry

CHAPTER 5

A Cultural Legacy:
The Pipers' Club and the 4th Battalion

The Pipers' Club is a unique association and is responsible for passing on an unbroken piping tradition from the 19th century to the present day. Founded in 1900, its origins are tied up with the Gaelic Revival, which focused interest on all aspects of our culture, including music.

A close examination of the Pipers' Club *Minute Book* (1900-04) reveals that many of its members were also members of the Gaelic League and the Irish Volunteers. Perhaps its most famous member is Éamonn Ceannt, the 1916 signatory. Ceannt was an Uilleann piper [and a War piper] and served as secretary of the Club until his marriage to the Club's treasurer, Áine Brennan.

As the Gaelic Revival gained momentum pipers were sought after to showcase the 'Gaelic' instrument at various functions. An entry signed in the *Second Minute Book* of the Pipers' Club, dated the 14th of October 1913, is a request from Pádraig Pearse via Éamonn Ceannt for pipers to play at a Feis in aid of St. Enda's School.

Following the Easter Rising and the subsequent War of Independence and Civil War, the Club became defunct through much of the 1920s and 1930s. However, piping continued in Dublin among certain families: the Rowsome, Potts, Ennis, Seery and Brophy families being the most prominent.

William Rowsome's son Leo was instrumental in reviving the Pipers' Club when it moved to 14 Thomas Street in the late 1940s. An outstanding Uilleann piper of national repute and one of a diminishing number of pipe makers, Rowsome taught the Uilleann pipes to a new generation –

Éamonn Ceannt performing on Uilleann Pipes.

including Paddy Moloney, Liam O'Flynn and Gay McKeon – thereby ensuring the continuity of the tradition.

14 Thomas Street proved a most suitable location. The building was the headquarters of the 4th Battalion of the Irish Volunteers and Old IRA; it was named Árus Ceannt after its former Commandant, Éamonn Ceannt. The premises were obtained through the influence of members of the 4th Battalion, including Oscar Nevin, whose daughter, Betty, became one of Rowsome's pupils and a proficient piper.

Thomas Street itself had many links over the years with traditional music. The pipe-maker, Coyne, had his premises there from 1840–1861 and Mrs. Kenny, who was known as the 'Queen of the Irish Fiddlers', lived nearby. Prominent musicians from the area included the Potts and McKenna families and pipers Dan O'Dowd and Tommy Reck. The renowned music collector, Breandán Breathnach, grew up in the locality.

The Saturday night sessions at 14 Thomas Street were legendary. It was a Mecca for any visiting musician or singer in Dublin. In 1951 Comhaltas Ceoltóirí Éireann (CCÉ) was established by the Pipers' Club and in 1972 it moved to Monkstown the new headquarters where the Pipers' Club continue their Saturday sessions. Thus ended an era of fantastic Club sessions in the South inner city. Breandán Breathnach, Sean Potts and more recently, Gay McKeon, a former pupil of Leo Rowsome, have also pioneered developments through Na Píobairí Uilleann (founded in 1968), which has resulted in more people playing Uilleann pipes world-wide than ever before. The current healthy state of Uilleann piping, therefore, can be traced back in part to Éamonn Ceannt, the 4th Battalion and 14 Thomas Street.

Mick O'Connor[53]
Traditional Musician, The Liberties

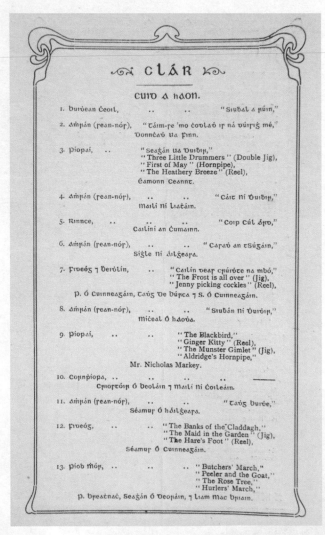

Programme from 1906 Pipers Festival, Gresham Hotel, showing Éamonn Ceannt's performance pieces. Courtesy National Library of Ireland.

Epilogue

"It was hard to realise it was the last leave-taking"

"After the fight on Thursday... [at the South Dublin Union]"... **Seosamh Ó Dubhláin** relates "it was observed that a picture of the Crucifixion hanging on the wall, opposite the windows was left untouched although the wall all round was torn with bullet marks...

All was quiet on Friday but we could hear the heavy guns firing on O'Connell Street... With the exception of very slight sniping Saturday was quiet...

Nothing happened on Sunday until after midday when Commandant Tom McDonagh accompanied by one of the Fathers from the Church of St. Mary of the Angels, Church Street, carrying a white. flag, approached the building and was admitted. They remained for some time in conversation with Commandant Ceannt. On their departure the Commandant called us together, told us of the unconditional surrender of Headquarters in order to save the lives of the citizens; of his discussion with McDonagh and their decision to agree to an unconditional surrender. Several questions were asked as to what that meant, which he answered. He then said, "If you decide against it, we can continue the fight, and get away to the mountains, but I recommend the surrender as we have won what we fought for. You may not see it now but you will see it later". On his recommendation the surrender was agreed to. He then said, "You men will get a double journey, but we, the leaders, will get a single journey". He then told us to collect all our guns and belongings and line up in front of the Nursing Home within half an hour...

We lined up as instructed by Commandant Ceannt, were numbered off by him, 42 of us, and awaited the arrival of the British military. After a short period a single senior British Officer walked in, approached Ceannt and said: "I see you are getting your men together". Ceannt answered, "No I have them together". Certainly the British Officer looked surprised at the small number. Ceannt gave us the order and moved off in front of us, accompanied by the British Officer to Marrowbone lane. Ceannt and the British Officer went into the Distillery and after some time led out that section of the Volunteers and members of Cumann na mBan, who fell in on our rere, and we continued our march to Bride Road. There we got the order from the British military, "Leave down all your equipment on the ground", and were marched to the opposite side of the road. A British car came along collecting all arms. We were surrounded by British soldiers and marched to Richmond Barracks."[54]

Editors' Entry

In *her* submission to the Bureau of Military History made in 1922, **Lily O'Brennan**, sister of Éamonn Ceannt's wife, Áine, wrote of the last hours in Marrowbone Lane when:

"On Sunday morning, Commandant Ceannt sent a dispatch to Capt Murphy. He had beaten the military from the Union; they were timid of advancing and he had made plans to come out. On receiving the Commandant's note, the Capt paraded his men, and gave them the news from the Union. He said it might be necessary in case of provisions giving out and they having to remain there to go on ½ or or perhaps no rations – he asked were they prepared to go on and fight – to the end thus. The answer was a glorious shout – all were prepared.

That afternoon Fr. Augustine and Thomas MacDonagh came with the news. They had seen Commandant Ceannt and he had agreed to the surrender. The Capt was to prepare his men. Ceannt would march with his men to the Distillery there to be joined by the balance of the battalion and thence to Patrick's Park. When the men heard the news they broke into tears and it is a hard thing to see men crying – well immediately Commd. Ceannt arrived. He had no cap on; his uniform was slightly torn; his face pale and I read in it the certain knowledge he then possessed of the fate in store for him.

He handed me a small purse for his wife – I asked him what was I to do. He said "go home". I asked would I take my bike – he said "yes". Those were the last words between us."[55]

Editors' Entry

Annie O'Brien also recalled *her* reaction to events immediately following the surrender when:

"Thinking the men would be taken away and we would not see them again, I went forward to where Con Colbert was standing to see whether there was anything he wanted me to do for him and also to get some souvenir in case I should never see him again. He was standing in rank with the other Volunteers with one sock in one hand and a piece of my mother's brown bread in the other. I asked him for a souvenir. "Here" he said, "these are all I have". He had, like all the others, been stripped of all his accoutrements. I did not take either of the articles he offered me, as I thought he might need the brown bread and the sock. He abominated holes in his socks and I mended a pair for him during the week and this was probably one of them."[56]

Editors' entry

Fr. Augustine Hayden, OFM, Cap[57]

In his witness statement to the Bureau of Military History, Fr. Augustine recounted that on 7th May 1916 he, together with Fr. Albert:

"had a busy day at Richmond Barracks and in the evening about 8 o'clock went to the house on North Circular Road where the officers were staying to inquire if our services would be required on the morrow. We were told that four were to be executed and, being ready when the car came in the early morning, we were quickly driven to Kilmainham. Here we were given the names of the condemned men – Micheal Mallin, Séan Heuston, Con Colbert and Éamonn Ceannt."[58]

Editors' Entry

Fr. Augustine Hayden, OFM, Cap

Con Colbert Memoriam Card. (Courtesy of Colbert Family.)

Éamonn Ceannt Memoriam Card. (Courtesy of Ceannt Family.)

He has lived a beautiful life and has
left a beautiful field,
He has sacrificed the hour to give service
for all time,
He has entered the company of the great
and with them he will be remembered forever.

Terence MacSwiney

"Brothers – 7th May 1916"[59]

At last the sentries—'Time's up please'—
made us stand for the final parting.
It was hard to realise
it was the last leave-taking.

~

Never demonstrative,
a simple handshake for us three
and a kiss for Aine
composed our last sad blessings.

~

On my way out the Commandant said,
no one had any right or reason to even suggest a reprieve,
that Éamonn was to be shot in the morning,
and kindly suggested my going back and telling him.

~

He was standing upright in his cell,
back partly to the door, hands in his pockets
apparently thinking
thinking
thinking.

~

I told him, his friend Father Augustine was coming.
He replied 'Oh, is that so?'
but in a tone that I since think meant
he knew all hope was gone.

~

Another handshake, still not a tremor,
and the door clangs between us.
Back into the rain and the night.
This was my last glance at my brother.
The candle was still burning.

Jessamine O'Connor
Great-Granddaughter of Richard Kent

Centenary Roll of Honour
4th Battalion
Dublin Brigade 1916

Recognising that there is no definitive Roll of Honour for the 4th Battalion, Dublin Brigade 1916, this Centenary Roll of Honour is compiled from various sources and endeavours to be as inclusive as possible.[60] The names are cited in alphabetical order.

The letter **d** against a name = denotes Killed in action in Easter Week 1916.

SOUTH DUBLIN UNION GARRISON

Arnold, James

Boylan, Thomas J.

Brugha, Cathal

Burke, James Joseph

Burke, William Francis (Frank) (Goban) = d

Byrne, Charles

Byrne, Joseph P.

Byrne, Liam

Carroll, Bartholomew Leo

Carroll, James

Ceannt, Éamonn

Coady, William

Condron, William (Liam)

Corrigan, William P.

Cosgrave, Philip (also in Marrowbone Lane)

Cosgrave, William T.

Coughlan, James John

Cullen, Thomas

Cunningham, Michael (also in Roe's Distillery)

Curran, William

Darcy, John Francis

Doherty, John Joseph)

Donelan, Brendan = d

Doolan, Joseph (Ó Dubhláin)

Downey, John (Seán)

Doyle, Gerald

Doyle, Peadar Seán

Evans, Robert J.

Fagan, Brian

Farrell, Michael

ffrench-Mullan, Douglas

Fogarty, James

Foran, James

Gannon, Laurence

Gibson, Edward (Edmund)

Gibson, Michael

Glynn, James (also in Roe's Malting House)

Graham, Thomas

Holland, Francis Michael

Howard, George

Irvine, George

Joyce, John Vincent

Kavanagh, Martin (also in Marrowbone Lane)

Keegan, Edward Laurence (Éamonn)

Kelly, Joseph Francis

Kenny, James

Kerr, Michael

Lynch, Michael Joseph

McCabe, John

McCarthy, Daniel

McDowell, William = d

McGlynn, John (Seán)

McKenna, John (Seán)

McMahon, Daniel Joseph

Maguire, James

Moloney, Patrick

Morrissey, James

Morrissey, Patrick S.

Murphy, John Christopher (Seán)

Murphy, William

SOUTH DUBLIN UNION GARRISON cont'd

O'Brien, Denis

O'Brien, Liam

O'Brien, Patrick

O'Brien, Stephen L

O'Byrne, William (Liam)

O'Flaherty, James

O'Flaherty, Martin

O'Flaherty, William (Liam Ó Flaithbheartaigh)

O'Gorman, John Patrick (also in Marrowbone Lane)

O'Loughlin, Patrick

O'Reilly, John

O'Reilly, Patrick

O'Reilly, Richard = d

O'Shaughnessy, John (Seán)

Owens, John (Seán) = d

Quinn, Charles

Quinn, James Joseph = d

Russell, James

Sears, David

Sweeney, Michael

Tracey, John (Seán)

Traynor, John (Seán) = d

Ward, Patrick (also in Roe's Malting House, Mt. Brown)

Ward, Patrick Joseph

Ward, Peter

Whelan, Richard

White, Michael [Mick]; (also in Marrowbone Lane)

Young, Éamonn

MARROWBONE LANE GARRISON

Adams, John

Bailey, Patrick J.

Bowman, Joseph

Bowman, William

Burke, Matthew

Bushell, Ellen Sarah

Butler, Christopher

Butler, Con

Byrne, Alphonsus (Alfie)

Byrne, Catherine (Kate)

Byrne, Denis

Byrne, Frank

Byrne, James (Seamus O'Broin)

Byrne, John Joseph

Byrne, Mary (May; Mrs. Mary Doyle)

Byrne, Michael

Byrne, Michael

Byrne, Winifred (Mrs. Winifred Somerville)

Carty, Thomas

Clarke, Joseph

Colbert, Con

Cooney, Áine (Mrs. Áine O'Brien)

Cooney, Eileen (Mr. Eileen Harbourne)

Cooney, Lily (Mrs. Lily Curran)

Corcoran, Brother Joseph Louis OFM

Corrigan, James

Cosgrave, Marcella

Cullen, John

Dempsey, William

Downey, John (Seán)

Downey, Joseph

Doyle, Christopher

Doyle, Joseph Francis

Doyle, Thomas J.

Dunne, Denis K.

Dunne, Patrick Joseph

Dunne, Peter (Peadar Ó Duinn)

Dwyer, Michael

Edwards, John

Feehan, James

Fitzpatrick, James

Foley, William

Gaskin, Francis

Gay, Thomas E. (Tomás Ernán)

Grehan, James

Harbourne, Patrick

Harbourne, Seán

Harmon, Patrick Joseph

Hegarty, Bridget (Mrs. Bridget Harmon)

Holland, Daniel

Holland, Robert

Holland, Walter Leo

Judge, John Patrick

MARROWBONE LANE GARRISON cont'd

Kavanagh, James Joseph

Keane, Liam

Kearney, Thomas

Kelly, Josephine
(Mrs. Josephine Greene)

Kennedy, Joseph P.

Kennedy, Margaret (Loo)

Kenny, James

Kenny, Kieran

Keogh, John

Keogh, Patrick

Kerrigan, Owen

Keys, John

Lamb, Patrick

Leigh, James

Liston, Michael

McCabe, Edward

McCabe, Peter

McCabe, Willliam

McCarthy, Patrick

McDermott, Louis
Bernard

McEvoy, Christopher
James

McGowan, Josie (Mac
Gabhan or McGavan)

McGrath, Joseph

McGrath, Patrick

McGrath, Patrick

McGrath, Seán

McKenna, Bernard

McNamara, Rose

McNamara, Sarah (or
MacNamara)

McNamee, James Kevin
(also in Watkins Brewery)

MacNeill, Dermot John
(Diarmuid)

McVeigh, James

MacNamee, Agnes

Marrinan, Edward

Mason, D.H.

Mason, Patrick

Meade, Daniel

Merriman, Edward

Moloney, John Joseph

Morgan, John

Mulcahy, Patrick

Mulhall, Lizzie

Mullally, Rosanna (Mrs.
Rosanna Farrelly)

Mullen, Martin

Mullen, Patrick

Murphy, Francis (also in
Roe's Distillery)

Murphy, James (Séamus
Ó Murchadha; also in
Roe's Distillery)

Murphy, Kathleen (Kate)

Murphy, Michael

Murphy, Thomas

Murray, Edward Joseph

Murray, Gabriel B.

Murray, Henry S.

Nevin, Fr. Eugene
(Served as Chaplain at
Marrowbone Lane)

Nolan, George Leo

Nolan, Thomas

Nugent, John
(also in Roe's Distillery)

Ó hAllmhuráin, Con
(Cornelius)

O'Brennan, Elizabeth M.
(Lily)

O'Brien, Denis
(Donnchadha Ó Briain)

O'Brien, Peter (Peadar)

Ó Broin, Pádraig

O'Byrne, Hugh

O'Byrne, John (Seán)

O'Carroll, Joseph

O'Connell, James (also in
Roe's Distillery)

O'Connor, Bernard

O'Flaherty,
Margaret (Cissie)
(Mrs. Margaret Timmons)

O'Gorman, John J.

O'Gorman, Joseph
(also in the South Dublin
Union)

O'Hanlon, Mary
(Molly, Máire)

O'Hanlon, Sheila (Sighle;
Mrs. Sighle Lynch)

O'Keeffe, Emily
(Mrs. Emily Hendley)

O'Keeffe, Josephine
(Josie)

O'Keefe, Josephine (Mrs.
Josephine McNamara)

O'Neill, Edward (Ned)

O'Neill, Joseph

O'Riordan, Michael

O'Rourke, Patrick

O'Shaughnessy, Theobald
(Ó Seachnasaigh)

Parcéir, Seosamh

Pender, Henry

Phelan, William

MARROWBONE LANE GARRISON cont'd

Phillips, John

Phillips, Matthew

Power, Arthur

Power, Joseph

Power, William (Liam; also in Watkins Brewery)

Quigley, Maria (Mary; Mrs. Mary Clince)

Quigley, Priscilla (Cilla; Mrs. Priscilla Kavanagh)

Rigney, Patrick Joseph

Roche, William

Saul, Frank

Saul, John [Jack]; (also in Roe's Malting House)

Smith, Michael

Spicer, Josephine

Teehan, James

Troy, Daniel

Troy, Paddy

Venables, Thomas

Walsh, James (Séamus Breathnach)

Walsh, James

Walsh, Patrick Joseph

Young, Patrick John (also in Watkins Brewery)

Young, Robert Martin (also in Watkins Brewery)

Young, Thomas

ROE'S DISTILLERY, MOUNT BROWN

Bowles, William Patrick

Byrne, George

Byrne, Patrick

Dowling, John (Seán)

Egan, Patrick

Fagan, William

Gaskin, Henry

Gaskin, Thomas

Gogan, John Gerard

Haran, D.

Horan, Daniel

Kelly, Frank

Kelly, Seán

Keogh, Martin

McCabe, Michael B.

McCarthy, Thomas

O'Brien, Laurence (Lorcan, Larry; also in Marrowbone Lane)

O'Brien, William (Liam; took up a position between Mt. Brown and Brookfield Road)

O'Grady, Charles Joseph

O'Hagan, James

O'Toole, John (also in Marrowbone Lane)

Quinn, George J.

Ward, Bernard

WATKINS BREWERY, ARDEE STREET.

Butler, James

Byrne, Christopher

Byrne, Patrick

Kavanagh, Thomas (also in Marrowbone Lane)

Kelly, William

McEvoy, Christopher

O'Hanlon, Luke Thomas

O'Neill, Michael (also in Marrowbone Lane)

O'Neill, Thomas (also in Marrowbone Lane)

ALSO IN 4TH BATTALION

Connolly, John (Na Fianna)

Dowling, Frank (Na Fianna)

Gunning, Charles (Na Fianna)

Murtagh, Laurence (Served at the Four Courts)

Murtagh, Thomas (Served at Dunboyne, Co. Meath)

O'Dowd, Dan (Na Fianna)

Comóradh 1916–2016: A Pictorial Record

Garrison Sites

Aerial photo of Watkins Brewery, post 1916. Courtesy BMH P 42/7.

Marrowbone Lane Distillery, post 1916. Courtesy BMH P 42/4.

Roe's Distillery (Malting House) looking down from Mount Brown, post 1916. Courtesy BMH P 42/38.

Front Gate, South Dublin Union (now St James's Hospital), post 1916. Courtesy libertiesdublin.ie.

Emerald Square

Pádraigín Clancy, Convenor, at the Marrowbone Lane Old Distillery Wall, on Easter Monday 2016. The Relatives' Group is hoping to have the wall preserved.

1916 Memorabilia

*1916 Medal
(Sheila O'Hanlon Lynch)*

*1966 Medal
(Pat Young)*

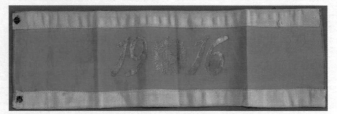

Mollie O'Hanlon's Cumann Na mBan 1916 Anniversary arm band

*Old Marrowbone Lane Wall plaque, erected 1940s –
now lost. Courtesy Liam Dempsey.*

*Plaque erected on Marrowbone Lane,
Old Distillery Wall, 24th April 2016.*

Comóradh 1966

1966 Some 4th Battalion Survivors:
South Dublin Union, Marrowbone Lane and Roe's Distillery 1916 Garrisons

Back Row L-R: Seán Harbourne, Séamus O'Flaherty, Frank Holland, Joe Doyle, Patrick Ward, Dan Horan, Patrick Egan Séamas Mac Coclain, Patrick J Dunne, Seán O'Shaughnessy, Liam O'Flaherty, Gerald Doyle, Francis Byrne, Patrick Harbourne.

Fourth Row L-R: James Byrne, Joe Clarke, Patrick Mason, George Nolan, Frank Kelly, James Corrigan, Seán Tracey, Thomas Graham, Arthur Power, Pádraig Ó Broin, Liam Mc Cabe, Edward Merriman,

Third Row L-R: Michael Cunningham, James J Burke, John Saul, Peter Ward, Patrick O'Loughlin, Joe Corcoran (Br Louis OSF), Thomas Kavanagh, Thomas J Doyle, Patrick J Rigney, Joseph O Connell, Patrick Byrne, Séamus Ó Murchadha.

Second Row L-R: Seán McGlynn, George Byrne, Mrs Winnefred Sommerville (Née Byrne), Mrs Rose Farrelly (née Mulally), Mrs Emily Handley (née O'Keefe), Mrs May Doyle (née Byrne), Mrs Maura Clince (née Quigley), Mrs Priscilla Kavanagh (née Quigley), Mrs Josephine McNamara (née O'Keefe), Mrs Eileen Harbourne (née Cooney), Mrs Sheila Lynch (née O'Hanlon), Mrs Margaret Timmons (née O'Flaherty), Patrick J Bailey.

First Row L-R: Joseph Doolan. Joseph Kennedy, Joseph O'Neill, Joseph Byrne, Henry Pender, John Adams, Patrick J Young, Christopher McEvoy, Thomas J Boylan.

Comóradh 2016

2016 Some 4th Battalion, Descendants
Gathered Inchicore College, 27th February 2016

Back Row L-R: Ken Saunders, Colm O'Dowd, Brian Cunningham, Don Butler, George Byrne, David Ceannt, John Morgan.

Third Row L-R: Pat Young, Don Farrell, Rita Tapley, Kate Hayes, Emily Smart, Niamh Lynch, Anne O'Gorman, Lorcan Dunne, Martine Smith, Ben Ó Broin.

Second Row L-R: Zita Bolton-Bowes, Darina O'Broin Tully, Séamus Ó Broin, Vera Murtagh, Sibéal Doolan (infront), Miriam Lynch, Clare Eager, Ursula Lynch (in front), Mary Gallagher, Eibhlín O'Shaughnessy Clancy, Bronagh O'Broin Stafford.

Front Row L-R: Fergus Brugha Bruton, Andrea Traynor Kavanagh, James Carberry and son Conor, Mary Gay-Smith, Pádraigín Ní Sheachnasaigh Clancy, Liam Cosgrave, Piaras Brugha Bruton, Mary Cosgrave, Seán Tapley.

4th Battalion Relatives Group at 1916 Commemorative Monument St James's Hospital, November 2015.

L-R: Fergus Brugha Bruton (grandson Cathal Brugha), David Ceannt (grandnephew Éamonn Ceannt), Piaras Brugha Bruton, Cathal MacSwiney Brugha (grandsons of Cathal Brugha) spontaneously singing 'God Save Ireland' on stairwell in Nurses Building, November 2015.

Section of crowd at State Wreath laying ceremony, Nurses Building, Easter Monday 2016.

Easter Monday, 2016 4th Battalion Relatives gather and lay wreaths, Marrowbone Lane.

Relatives group field trip with local historian Cathy Scuffil to Emerald Square, December 2015.

Unveiling of Plaque at Marrowbone Lane, Old Distillery Wall by Lord Mayor of Dublin, Críona Ní Dhálaigh, 24th April, 2016.